'The boundless things of nature attract me... I proceed very slowly, for nature reveals herself to me in very complex ways and there is endless progress to be made.'

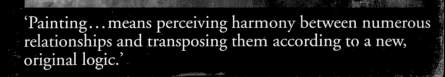

'Painting... means perceiving harmony between numerous relationships and transposing them according to a new, original logic.'

'For if the strong feeling for nature – which I assuredly
have  – is the necessary basis for all conception of art
upon which depend the greatness and beauty of all future

work, the knowledge of the means of expressing our emotion is no less essential and is only to be acquired through very long experience.'

'Light and shade are a relation of colours; the two principal accidentals differ not by dint of their general intensity but rather through their own specific sonority.'

'Shadow is a colour as light is, but less brilliant; light and shadow are only the relation of two tones.'

'There is no such thing as line or modelling, there are only contrasts. These are not contrasts of light and dark, but the contrasts given by the sensation of colour.'

'Modelling is the outcome of the exact relationship of tones. When they are harmoniously juxtaposed and complete, the picture develops modelling of its own accord.'

*P. Cezanne*

# CONTENTS

# CÉZANNE
## THE FIRST MODERN PAINTER

Michel Hoog

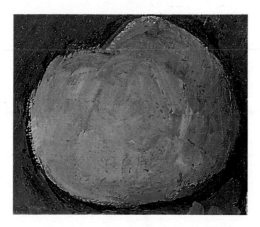

THAMES AND HUDSON

'The banker Cézanne does not see
    without fear
    Behind his desk a painter appear.'
It was with these words that a brilliant
schoolboy of Aix-en-Provence, who
occasionally wrote poetry, stated his
determination to become a painter
in spite of his father.

## CHAPTER 1
# YOUTH

Working from a photograph (a novelty in the early 1860s), Cézanne deliberately made himself look very unattractive (opposite). His yellow complexion, his staring eyes and his frown make him look quite Mephistophelian. Later self-portraits, which never portrayed him smiling, lacked the dramatic quality of this painting.

## Cézanne spends his childhood and youth quietly and studiously in Aix-en-Provence and the nearby region

Paul Cézanne, born on 19 January 1839, had two sisters, Marie and Rose. His father Louis-Auguste, who was born in 1798, had made enough money in the hat trade to found the only bank in Aix-en-Provence in 1848. He exerted his parental authority to the full when Paul chose to become an artist, but he does not seem to have been unduly severe with his children. Cézanne's mother, Elisabeth (née Aubert), an intelligent and lively woman about whom little is known, appears to have encouraged the artist and to have supported him when there were arguments between father and son.

Young Paul learned to read at the local primary school, then spent two years at the Ecole Saint-Joseph. Then he went into the first form of the Collège Bourbon at Aix as a boarder in 1852. He passed his baccalauréat with a 'quite good' grade in 1858. Cézanne left the lycée with an excellent knowledge of Latin, Greek, and ancient and French literature. He was able to compose poetry in Latin and French with great ease and several of his poems or fragments of plays, generally written in a bombastic tone and som ...mes a little racy, survive.

All his life Cézanne remained true to his humanist education. The man who rejected every tradition in painting had classical tastes in literature, read widely and was open to new approaches, such as Baudelaire's work.

## In 1852 Paul Cézanne comes to the aid of Emile Zola, who is persecuted by his schoolfriends. It is the beginning of forty years of friendship

Emile Zola (1840–1902) was a pupil in the lowest form. He was sickly, fatherless, badly short-sighted and was

This portrait of Marie Cézanne (below left), sister of the artist, is one of the very few portraits of women from Cézanne's early years (c. 1866). It was treated in a thick impasto applied with a palette knife. Cézanne liked this quick and somewhat crude technique. It went against received academic opinion and the smooth and over-polished painting practised by Ingres' students and taught at Aix.

There are some ten portraits of Uncle Dominique Aubert (above), brother of the artist's mother, who was a docile and obliging model for his nephew. Colour was applied with a palette knife over most of the canvas and sometimes even directly with the artist's fingers.

often bullied by his fellow students until Paul Cézanne, a 'big boy' from two forms above began to stand up for him. The day after Cézanne first intervened, Zola brought some apples as a present for his protector. Bonds were forged between these two children which were to last until 1886: both boys were to become famous.

There was a third boy at the Collège Bourbon, Baptistin Baille (1841–1918), a future student of the Ecole Polytechnique, and he, Cézanne and Zola made an inseparable trio. They spent their days off going for walks in the countryside around Aix and in the summer bathing in the river Arc. In a letter of 5 February 1861, written to Cézanne from Paris, Zola recalled these outings with nostalgia. 'Alas, no, I no longer wander the countryside, I no longer lose my way among the rocks of Le Tholonet and above all I no longer make my way

with a bottle in my game-bag to Baille's little estate, that unforgettable shooting-box reminiscent of wine.'

A good pupil who had won many prizes, Cézanne never complained about his school years, during which he gained his solid classical education. Above: the Collège Bourbon which became the Lycée Mignet. The town of Aix and its countryside formed the sole setting for Cézanne's childhood and youth. In the photograph (left), Saint-Jean-de-Malte's belfry marks the site of the Municipal School of Drawing, built on to the side of the church. The surrounding country was the scene of many of the artist's outings before providing him with the subject of his paintings.

### A city-dweller in love with the open air and music

Cézanne preferred the most secluded parts of the countryside round Aix. When asked his favourite smell in the family game Confidences, he replied 'the smell of the fields' and his favourite leisure activity, 'swimming'. Twice in letters to Emile Zola he recalled the same spot. In a letter of 9 April 1858 Cézanne wrote: 'Do you remember the pine that grew on the side of the Arc and leant its bushy head out over the chasm yawning at its feet? This pine which protected our bodies from the burning sun with its needles, ah! may the gods preserve it from the deadly blows of the woodcutter's axe!'

Cézanne showed a fondness for his birthplace and a feeling, not so common at this period when the philosophy of Jean-Jacques Rousseau (1712–78) was no longer fashionable, for nature, plants and bathing in the river. He differed here from his future fellow-Impressionists, who remained city-dwellers, Parisians by adoption, for

whom nature was for a long time identified with public gardens and with the orchards of the Ile-de-France.

Cézanne and his friends also amused themselves by playing music. In the 'Jolly Fellows' band founded by young Emile Zola, the future painter performed on the cornet, while Zola more modestly played the clarinet. When Cézanne went to live in Paris, he took his instrument with him. Zola, like most of the writers of

'No, I make off
Over the changing waves
As happily as
In years gone by,
When our agile arms
Like serpents swam
Over the gentle waves.
Goodbye, happy days
Seasoned with wine!
Lucky catches of huge fish!'

Paul Cézanne
Letter to Emile Zola
9 April 1858

his time, soon lost his enthusiasm for music but Cézanne – like Edouard Manet, Pierre-Auguste Renoir, Henri Fantin-Latour and Gauguin – was devoted to it. Cézanne admitted his admiration for Richard Wagner (1813–83) at a time when the German composer was unpopular in France. At the end of his life Cézanne even stopped going to vespers because the assistant priest in the cathedral played the organ so badly.

The son of an Italian immigrant, Louis-Auguste Cézanne (below), founded the Cézanne and Cabassol bank in 1848. It was to bring him wealth.

**Following his father's wishes, the young man enrols, without much enthusiasm, at the university of Aix to study law. But he is drawn in another direction**

Louis-Auguste Cézanne was a self-taught man. By hard work and intelligence he had become very well-off. He hoped that his son, after brilliant further studies, would turn to a legal career and become a lawyer or a judge. What a step-up it would be for Louis-Auguste, who was despised by the aristocracy of Aix – he owed his fortune to the hat trade and, it was said, to money-lending – to see his son sitting in the court of appeal in Aix-en-Provence!

The young Paul Cézanne seemed to accept the idea, initially at any rate, of following this classic 19th-century route to social advancement. But neither the bank nor the law interested him and little by little he turned towards that most discredited of all professions in the bourgeois mind: that of the artist.

'I shall get an idea of the dangers that painting runs when I see your attempts,' said his art-teacher Joseph Gibert (below) on seeing Cézanne's canvases at the first Impressionist exhibition in 1874.

### In 1857, before finishing his secondary education, Cézanne enrols in the Municipal School of Drawing in Aix

His art-teacher was Joseph Gibert, who, following a practice common in the 19th century, was not only director of the drawing academy but also curator of the local Musée Granet. His teaching, supplementing the instruction of the Collège courses in drawing, certainly did not show great originality. Gibert passed on to Cézanne a certain know-how through the methods then in use, especially the copying of casts of antique works and the study of live models. The painter was to maintain good relations with Gibert and would show

deference to him, even though Gibert's authoritarian ways and out-of-date art would have justified a certain hostility on his part. Should this attitude be explained by the respect that Cézanne always showed towards those in some form of authority? Or was he grateful to Gibert for having taught him the rudiments of art?

During 1859 and 1860 Cézanne was simultaneously keeping up both his law studies and a real professional painting course at the Municipal School. In 1859 he won second prize for a figure painting and his father allowed him to continue. The young student avoided his seven years' military service thanks to the purchase of a 'replacement', a system widely practised at the time.

## The first known work of the young Cézanne is his decoration of the Jas de Bouffan, a property acquired by his father in 1859

In purchasing this large 18th-century house in a beautiful park two kilometres from the centre of Aix, Louis-Auguste Cézanne was trying to gain social acceptance by falling into line with the customs of the great families of Aix. The young Paul loved this house and stayed and worked there frequently. The imposing building and the trees in the park can be seen in many of his paintings and watercolours.

The decoration of the salon at the Jas de Bouffan was undertaken soon after the house was bought with his father's consent. The mural consisted of an allegory of the four seasons, to which Cézanne later added other subjects: one of these was a portrait of his father. *The Four Seasons* panels no doubt helped Louis-Auguste decide to let his son 'go up to Paris', a step which had first been authorized in 1860, then quickly rescinded and at last agreed on in 1861.

The panels of *The Four Seasons* were detached from the wall and acquired by the art dealer Ambroise Vollard: he offered them to the Musée du Petit Palais in Paris. The panels show female figures in the style of hand-painted wallpapers or romantic screens. *Autumn* (right) and *Spring* (far right) exhibit elegant, graceful silhouettes and recall Sandro Botticelli (c. 1445–1510) in their poses. These beginner's paintings are not without ambition. The incisive drawing, the clarity of the contours, the elongated arms all explain why Cézanne ironically signed the picture 'Ingres'. Ingres (1780–1867) was then the obligatory reference point of all academic teaching.

## In the 19th century, to go up to Paris is the dream of every ambitious young man

The centralization of administrative power and the concentration of all the big schools and the big cultural institutions in Paris explained this longing. To it must be added the freedom from the moral strictness of provincial life, as opposed to the reputation ascribed to Parisian bohemians for a free and easy life. This applied particularly to the world to which young Cézanne dreamed of belonging, namely that of the arts. The provincial schools – with the exception of Lyons – were extremely undistinguished, not to say moribund, and all the great artistic battles since Romanticism and Realism took place in Paris. The Salons and the controversies they aroused every year, the great state commissions, the construction programme of the Second Empire, Gustave Courbet's special exhibition of 1855, of all these only distant echoes reached the provinces. It was in Paris, and in Paris alone that a young artist could train and make his mark. Wasn't Paris the capital of the arts? Didn't it attract artists from all over the world?

## 'I would want...to risk all to gain all, and not hesitate any longer between two such different choices for my future, between art and the law'

Cézanne, who felt strongly that he had a vocation as an artist, also dreamed of going to Paris. Added to his ambitions as a painter was the longing to free himself from his family and its constraints.

Zola, his junior, who had been in Paris since 1858, wrote to him regularly and encouraged him to follow his true calling. In a letter of July 1860 Zola wrote: 'Is painting only a whim that came up and seized you one fine day when you were bored? Is it only a pastime, a subject of conversation, a pretext for not working at the

This sketch of people gathered round a table is the precursor of *The Cardplayers*. It was the subject of a letter to Emile Zola (above right) written on 17 January 1859, entitled 'Death reigns in this place'.

law? If it is like this, then I understand why you are behaving in this way: you do well not to push things to extremes and not to make new family troubles for yourself. But if painting is your vocation – and I have always thought of it in this way – if you think you are capable of doing well after having worked hard, then you are an enigma to me, a sphinx, an impossible and impenetrable mystery.' Zola came back to Aix in the summer of 1860 and no doubt his urging had something to do with Cézanne's decision to go up to the capital.

Delacroix, who died in 1863, was the Great Man for the painters of this later generation. However, while Degas (1834–1917), Gauguin (1848–1903) and Renoir (1841–1919) succeeded in reconciling their admiration for him with admiration for his old rival Ingres, Cézanne several times showed open dislike for Ingres and his disciples. Below: the portrait of Delacroix (1864–6) by Cézanne.

## 'I am working calmly, eating well and sleeping likewise'

In November 1862, after one false start, Cézanne settled in Paris, where he led a simple and studious life. He frequently worked at the Atelier Suisse or at home and often visited museums. He attended the annual Salon with much interest. From 1863 on he was a frequent visitor to the Louvre, where he copied the works of art: he also went to the Luxembourg museum, which was reserved for living artists, and discovered the works of someone who was to become one of the painters he most admired: Eugène Delacroix (1798–1863). *The Massacre at Chios* and *Dante and Virgil in the Inferno* were hung side by side with the works of disciples of Ingres. No doubt he went to pay his devotions at the chapel of the Saints-Anges at Saint-Sulpice and perhaps he tried to see the decorations in the Chamber of Deputies. He painted in the open air, sometimes in Paris, more often when he went to live for some time in the surrounding countryside.

Mon cher ami,

Je t'autorise à prendre ma clef chez le concierge.

Paul Cézanne

This fine *Head of an Old Man* (1865–8), a more sensitive and elaborate portrait than the one of Uncle Dominique, was painted over another work. It is possible to make out at the bottom right, going across the picture, a kind of procession which has been covered over by Cézanne. Below left: *Medea and Her Children* (1879–82) after Delacroix. Below right: a sketch (c. 1868–71) in the spirit of Honoré Daumier.

Cézanne went to the cafés much less frequently than his fellow-artists and preferred the company of his friends from Aix – Emile Zola, Numa Coste, Antony Valabrègue and Achille Emperaire. He was not, however, unsociable, he knew how to be good fun and to share in the free and easy life in the country inns, for example at Bennecourt, near Mantes, in 1866. Several times he was invited for a few days to Zola's house at Médan.

**Cézanne is lucky and does not come up against the extreme poverty and lack of money suffered by other artists**

He was able to live thanks to the allowance that his father paid him and that his mother no doubt discreetly supplemented. 'My good family, excellent, it must be said, in other respects, is for a poor painter who has never known what to do, perhaps a little miserly. It is a minor fault and doubtless excusable in the provinces.' He had simple tastes which he never abandoned even when he came into his father's fortune. Louis-Auguste hoped that his son would either become discouraged or else would make a success by following the more acceptable paths: the Ecole des Beaux-Arts, the Prix de Rome.... Neither of these hopes were realized. The young Cézanne continued, but as an independent painter, failing the entrance examination for the Ecole and suffering repeated refusals from the Salon.

When he stayed at Aix, he was sure of bed and board at the family home. Apart from his need to steep himself in the atmosphere of Aix again, perhaps board and lodging were additional motives for his frequent return to the region. Cézanne no doubt suffered from being dependent and from unfavourable criticism of his work, but his attitude to his father combined deference with determination to protect his vocation.

Antony Valabrègue, a poet and art-critic (above), was a member of the little group of men from Aix who were fond of frequenting Parisian cafés and formed a circle round Cézanne and Zola. Cézanne, the surly provincial, felt ill at ease at the Café Guerbois, which symbolized the spirit of Paris; he fell silent and reacted violently when he ran into opinions opposed to his own. One evening he even provoked Manet: 'I won't shake hands, M. Manet, I haven't washed for a week.'

## 'I cannot accept the unjustified criticism of fellow-artists whom I have not myself expressly asked to appraise me'

Cézanne came up against the Salon jury for the first time in 1863, when he sent in a painting that was rejected. It was the year when the jury proved so severe that Napoléon III, facing a wave of protest, decided that a Salon des Refusés should be opened. Cézanne found himself there, along with his friends Camille Pissarro (1830–1903) and Armand Guillaumin (1841–1927) and also Henri Fantin-Latour (1836–1904), James Whistler (1834–1903) and especially Edouard Manet (1832–83), who caused a great scandal with his painting *Déjeuner sur l'Herbe.*

The experiment of the Salon des Refusés was not repeated in the next few years in spite of a haughty letter written by Cézanne on 19 April 1866 to Count de Nieuwerkerke, the Director of Fine Arts, in which he expressed his scorn for the jury of the Salon and the right of an artist to show his works to the public. 'I want to appeal to the public and have an exhibition all the same. My wish does not seem to me to be at all outrageous, and, if you were to ask all those painters in my position,

Painters rejected by the Salon had no chance of making their name. In 1863 the 'rejected' managed to form an exhibition in a side-wing. This show was strongly ridiculed, as can be seen in the caricature published in a newspaper of the time (below centre): 'My son! Take off your cap! Honour the courage of these unfortunates!'

Manet's *Déjeuner sur l'Herbe* (1863), which takes up the theme in *Fête Champêtre* (c. 1510) in the Louvre (then attributed to Giorgione), of a nude female in a landscape in the company of men wearing ordinary town clothes, was judged to be immoral.

they would all reply that they rejected the jury and that they wished to take part in one way or another in an exhibition which should perforce be open to every genuine working artist.'

**From his first works on, the young painter tries his hand at all styles and his output before 1870 is quite difficult to classify**

Cézanne himself destroyed many of his paintings. Very few of those that remain are dated and the countless historians who have studied them disagree about the chronology and the interpretation of the scenes represented.

The style is not consistent. Some successes bear witness to a thoroughly mastered craft, while others give the impression of clumsiness.

Technique and subject matter are fused in Cézanne. In violent scenes (above, *The Murder* of c. 1867–8) and in the slightly caricatured early portraits, he worked very quickly. The thick brushstrokes are clearly visible and there is frequent use of the palette knife. Peaceful still-lifes are worked with a smoother and more thoughtful brush.

Paul Alexis (1847–1901), who also came from Aix-en-Provence, was Zola's disciple and for a little while his secretary. He figured in *Médan Soirées* (1880), a joint collection of short stories of the Naturalist school. Cézanne here (left) has given him the part of the reader. This composition brings to mind Manet's double portraits. The painting was left unfinished, a very rare occurrence for Cézanne, who preferred to destroy works with which he was not satisfied. Zola's figure, barely sketched in, creates a striking contrast with its white patch against the rest of the canvas. The portrait of Alexis, seated and in profile, calls to mind Manet's famous picture of Zola (below), which was painted only a year or two earlier in 1868. The painting was discovered in Zola's attic many years after his death.

This is caused by faulty technique, haste of execution or deliberate caricature. Cézanne complained about his lack of ability and difficulty in realizing his vision on canvas.

His themes are very varied. Even before 1870, Cézanne was painting still-lifes made up of familiar objects, portraits (almost exclusively masculine), landscapes, allegorical figures and, contrasting strongly with these traditional themes, some violent and gruesome scenes such as *The Autopsy, The Abduction, The Orgy, Afternoon in Naples* and *The Temptation of Saint Anthony.* He tried out every style, whereas most painters, not only his contemporaries, favoured one, or at most two.

## The painter twice painted his father reading the newspaper

Did Louis-Auguste Cézanne really pose or did his son take the opportunity of painting him while he was hardly moving? The older of the two portraits was given a place of honour in the Salon of the Jas de Bouffan, between the allegories *Summer* and *Winter.*

Three or four years later, the other picture of his father showed the mastery acquired by Cézanne in Paris. This time, the masses were cleverly disposed in space. Light and shade were handled with care, especially on the face and the armchair (which appeared in other pictures). Cézanne's work here is close to Monet's and Renoir's, at a moment which formed the prelude to Impressionism.

Cézanne was really being kind in revealing the name of the paper his father was reading. It was not his father's usual newspaper, but *L'Evénement,* which had in April and May 1866 published some very aggressive reviews of the Salon (a 'mass of mediocrity'). Using a pseudonym, Zola wrote reviews that caused a scandal; Villemessant, the editor of the paper, suspended publication of the articles and fired Zola.

One of the young painter's still-lifes is hung behind the armchair – *Still-life with Sugar Bowl, Pears and Blue Cup* (1863–5) – which has been altered slightly. His art was thus allowed in to the parental home. But should we give a symbolic meaning to the fact that Louis-Auguste has turned his back on a work by his son?

Cézanne's originality lies in his working method – the painting was largely executed with a palette knife – and in the strength of contrast between the pure whites, greys and blacks. Cézanne also tried out this contrast in his still-lifes.

The most monumental portrait of this time is, apart from the one of his father, the strange likeness of Achille Emperaire. He was a painter from Aix with whom Cézanne had worked at the Atelier Suisse and to whom Cézanne remained very attached. On the deformed body of a dwarf the man had 'a magnificent head like that of a Van Dyck cavalier'. Cézanne executed several preparatory drawings for this picture, devoid of any caricature, whereas the oil painting emphasized the ridiculous and pitiable side of the individual.

This picture was bought in turn by two painters, Emile Schuffenecker, a friend of Paul Gauguin, and Eugène-Guillaume Boch, one of Van Gogh's models. Cézanne in his later years wished to destroy it, but it has always claimed attention even if only for its size and its intrinsic quality of caricature. It was painted a little before 1870, as Cézanne tried to get it admitted to the Salon that year. The painter was then on a quest for a style or, as he himself said, for a 'formula', a voluntary quest relying more at that moment on the study of the past than on analysis of his sensations. The frontal viewpoint, the gaudy colours, the note of caricature, the inscription in printed characters were a mixture of the archaic with the sign-painter's craft. The armchair Emperaire is sitting in is to be found again in his father's portrait and, though empty, in *The Overture to Tannhäuser* of c. 1869–70 (see pp. 38–9).

At the same time he undertook a new and enormous composition on a wall of the Jas de Bouffan, *Christ in Limbo* and *Mary Magdelene*. An old photograph shows how this work originally looked and it has to be admitted that the left-hand part of it (*Christ in Limbo*) fits together badly with the right-hand part (*Mary Magdelene*). It has been suggested that they constitute two quite separate compositions or else that the painting was meant to be extended on the right and that *Mary Magdelene* was to have formed part of an *Entombment* which was never painted.

### 'No painting done indoors, in the studio, will ever be as good as anything done in the open air'

In a letter to Zola written on 19 October 1866, Cézanne explained his views on *plein-air* painting: 'When out-of-door scenes are represented, the contrast between the figures and the ground is astonishing and the landscape is magnificent. I see some superb things and I shall have to make up my mind only to do things out-of-doors.'

The landscapes of this period do not herald Impressionism; rather they bring to mind Gustave Courbet (1819–77) or the Barbizon school: dark colours with deep blacks and greens, the relief suggested in a rather academic way by a succession of parallel planes.

Cézanne's subject matter, although varied and containing most of the traditional themes, did not include any religious scene other than (below) *Christ in Limbo* and *Mary Magdelene* (also known as *Sorrow*); *The Temptation of Saint Anthony* can hardly be counted as such. Christ is copied from a painting by Sebastiano del Piombo (c. 1485–1547) in the Prado museum, and the Magdelene recalls a painting by Domenico Feti (1589–1623) in the Louvre. Originally these two figures hung side by side on a wall in the Jas de Bouffan.

Fortuné Marion
(photograph above),
a friend from Aix-en-
Provence, went with
Cézanne on excursions
into the countryside
where he found his
inspiration. He was a
geologist who had also
taken up painting
himself. *Marion and
Valabrègue Setting out to
Paint from Nature* of
1866 (left), in which the
two friends are dressed
for outdoor painting,
was Cézanne's first
manifesto for the *plein-
air* school.

It is difficult to see if
the heavy forms in
this landscape (1865–7)
are trees or rocks. Man
is absent; the artist
portrays a wild primitive
nature with the same
energy with which he
paints his models' faces.

*The Orgy* (left) of c. 1870 is a canvas of exceptional size. Cézanne was insistent it should appear in his first one-man show at Ambroise Vollard's in 1895, just when his art had taken a completely different direction.

**Orgies, drunken revels, abductions, these themes of many of his early paintings reveal a strongly sensual temperament**

Little is known, however, of the emotional life of the young Cézanne: the letters contain allusions to student love-affairs, which perhaps remained platonic. *The Orgy*, one of the most elaborate canvases of the period, groups people, either naked or in fantasy costumes, around a table which seems to be overturned: they are entwined in utter confusion. Cézanne, who had mastered the distribution of mass and space on canvas, has deliberately given this composition an agitated feeling of violence. His range of colours was very bright, indeed shocking for the time: his light greens, his reds and the great blue sky contrast sharply with the range of tragic blacks, dark greens and Prussian blue of the other paintings of this period, as though he intended the violence of the colours to match that of the subject. In the same vein there are several little pictures which, by the standards of his own time, would have been called pornographic if he had been able to exhibit them. These erotic subjects disappeared and his work settled down around 1870, when he met Hortense Fiquet.

⁶ One of his most remarkable paintings of this period [1866–70] was done at Zola's house in the Rue de la Condamine, and Cézanne made his friend a present of it. This painting, *The Abduction* [or *The Rape*], dated 1867, even though not reaching the 12 or 15 feet [4 or 5 m] of which the artist had dreamed, measures 35 by 46 inches [0.90 m by 1.17m]. It represents a large green plain done in vivid, comma-like strokes that make it look like troubled water. Against this a nude giant strangely bronzed stands out. In his arms he carries a pale woman with blue-black hair; from her hips falls a dark blue drape. The harmony between her white skin and the bronze of the man, surrounded by the blue material and the green plain, is harsh. In the background, in front of a white cloud, arises a mountain vaguely reminiscent of Sainte-Victoire. At the left two little pink bodies of young girls enliven the composition.⁹

John Rewald
*Cézanne: A Biography*
1986

## Cézanne also goes in for what was then considered a minor genre: still-life

A very popular genre in the 18th century, still-life was neglected in Neo-classical and Romantic times. Francisco Goya (1746–1828), Théodore Géricault (1791–1824) and Eugène Delacroix went in for it in a very minor way, but it was only towards 1860, doubtless because of renewed interest in the genre painter Jean-Baptiste-Siméon Chardin (1699–1779), whose works had just been shown in a major exhibition, that strong and independent personalities such as Gustave Courbet, François Bonvin, Edouard Manet, Antoine Vollon and Henri Fantin-Latour found still-life a favourite genre for their experiments.

Cézanne was similar to Manet in using rich blacks, greys and white, and in the very unorthodox effect of lighting from the front.

Some still-lifes, like the one he put behind his father reading the newspaper, were executed with a palette knife. The crude strokes, the accentuated contrast between light and dark, and the simplicity of the composition connect this group of works to a few portraits where Cézanne openly expressed the violence of his temperament.

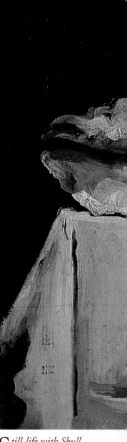

*Still-life with Skull and Candlestick* (above left) of 1865–7 is typical of the early still-lifes where the choice of objects is often traditional but the technique and the effect of the light are determinedly modern.

Others show less bold treatment and more ambitious construction. However, their precise date is too uncertain to be able to state that they are later works. The structure of the composition is sometimes based on a pattern of squares, as in *Still-life with a Black Clock,* where the folds of the napkin are depicted with care. In other cases, the artist arranges the space between objects somewhat in the manner of certain 17th-century still-lifes.

The first still-lifes were almost exclusively devoted to fruit, though it was no longer to be the only subject. Cézánne introduced other objects which were chosen

The black clock, painted without hands by Cézanne, belonged to Zola. The tablecloth falls in four rigid folds, recalling the rockface of the quarries in the country round Aix.

not only for the simplicity of their form or the clarity of their surface, but also for their significance: a clock without hands, shells, an almost burnt-out candle and above all, many times over, skulls, those gruesome props, explicit symbols of the shortness of life which brings these paintings close to the 'Vanitas' of the 17th century.

## Cézanne shows that he can link his figures together in plastic form

With *The Overture to Tannhäuser* he succeeded in a kind of composition that many painters, and not only minor ones, have had difficulty in mastering: the scene with two figures. Those who, like Renoir, manage to express human feelings of love, of friendship, of sympathy or even a simple, fleeting relationship between two people are rare. Manet (with a few exceptions), Degas and especially Fantin-Latour usually only finished up juxtaposing two lonely people.

Cézanne, devoted to music like many painters and an admirer of Wagner, painted three different versions of an interior showing a young girl playing the piano which he called *Overture to Tannhäuser*. He painted these canvases in 1866, long after the performances of *Tannhäuser* at the Paris Opera had been deliberately disrupted.

The composition of *The Overture to Tannhäuser* (below and detail, right), is rigidly structured by a series of right angles (the armchair, the uprights of the sofa, the chair, the pianist's arms, the piano itself). All the elements of the picture are parallel or perpendicular to the canvas plane. A gentle diffused light, subdued colours, delicately blended reflections on the armchair give the scene the poetic quality of a Vermeer or a Chardin. Touches of glaze make the whites and greys vibrate.

### In 1869 Cézanne meets an artists' model of nineteen in Paris who is to become – much later – Madame Cézanne

The painter lived with Hortense Fiquet without the knowledge of his family or at least of his father. The first paintings where her beautiful oval face can definitely be recognized date from after 1871. She was to become Cézanne's most available and most patient model.

In the spring of 1870, Cézanne's offering was once again rejected by the jury of the Salon. On 31 May he was a witness at Zola's wedding in Paris, and then set off for Aix.

When the Franco-Prussian war, which led to the fall of the Second Empire, broke out, Cézanne did not rush

'Courbet, Manet, Monet and all of you who paint with a knife, a paintbrush, a brush or any other instrument, you are all outmoded! May I present your master: M. Cézannes [sic].' Cézanne is here (above) portrayed by Stock, the caricaturist, with his two paintings, the *Portrait of Achille Emperaire* and a nude, now lost, both of which were rejected by the Salon jury of 1870. This caricature appeared in Stock's Paris weekly in the spring of 1870.

Female portraits, rare in the early years, became much more numerous from the moment when Cézanne met Hortense Fiquet in 1869. Left: *Madame Cézanne in the Red Armchair* (1877).

to rejoin the army. He went to live with Hortense Fiquet, still unbeknownst to his father, in a house which had been rented by his mother at l'Estaque and which was often to serve him – significantly – as a refuge. The police looked for him in vain at Aix. The lack of patriotic feeling in Cézanne 'the deserter' is difficult to interpret.

Totally absorbed in his passion for art, Cézanne was embarrassingly indifferent towards other people, and during his whole life never showed the slightest interest in civic matters.

About thirty kilometres from Aix, l'Estaque was then a simple village on the shore of the Mediterranean. Cézanne often depicted its picturesque features with the hills falling straight into the sea.

Unfortunately, not one of the known paintings can be dated with any certainty from the first stay. Prolonged observation of the sea certainly contributed to the lightening of Cézanne's palette and to his interest in the study of reflections: he was hardly concerned with any of these matters before this time, but they had for several years preoccupied his companions Pissarro, Monet and Renoir. This change only appeared in Cézanne's painting later, around 1871 to 1872.

This uninviting landscape (1870) of the outskirts of Aix, where the railway cutting opens up like a wound, is dominated by the Mont Sainte-Victoire. It was the first, and for a long time the only, painting Cézanne made of this mountain near Aix which was later to inspire him so often.

After his stay at l'Estaque, Cézanne went back to Paris. Pissarro was at Pontoise, gathering round him young revolutionary painters. Cézanne joined him in 1873, accompanied by Hortense Fiquet and their son Paul, who was born in 1872. Between Paris, Pontoise and Auvers-sur-Oise, some ten years of serenity followed the long period of anxiety and searching of his youth. Cézanne seemed to have found his feet.

CHAPTER 2

## THE IMPRESSIONIST PERIOD

Impressionism has its own atmosphere: that of the Ile-de-France and the Channel coast. The countryside of the Oise contributed to Cézanne's development. His palette lightened and the violent contrasts of blacks and whites made way for bright colours. Right and detail left: *The Little Houses at Auvers* (c. 1873–4).

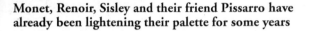

### Monet, Renoir, Sisley and their friend Pissarro have already been lightening their palette for some years

Their landscapes of the Ile-de-France and Normandy broke away from the patterns set by previous generations. These painters became more and more interested in the effects of light on nature, bodies, clouds, water. They discovered that shadow was not uniformly brown or black and that light changed the colour of objects. They abandoned literary, historical or narrative subjects and instead adopted a modern portfolio of subjects, predominantly outdoor scenes, and, in Monet's case, landscapes with water.

Such experiments could only be carried out using a suitable technique. They invented it: colour laid on with small hatched brushstrokes, a jumble of different colours on the canvas itself, elimination of browns and blacks and quick execution out of doors, almost always at the scene being painted. This revolutionary approach earned the small group of artists (who had not yet been called Impressionists) the mockery of both the uncomprehending critics and the public.

### Cézanne joins the group of innovators only in 1873

When he came to live in Pontoise in 1872, Cézanne had already known Pissarro for seven or eight years and Guillaumin for even longer. He was familiar with the

The Impressionist movement was not born in a day, the result of improvisation or a chance discovery, as Monet and Renoir later lead people to believe. Eugène Boudin (1824–98) had taught these painters to transpose the most delicate transformations of light. He also taught Manet to abandon anecdotal and narrative painting. For about ten years, Pissarro the master, and also Monet, Renoir, Guillaumin and others had been working in the same direction. Above from left to right, Renoir (by Frédéric Bazille), Guillaumin (by Cézanne), Pissarro (photograph), Sisley (by Renoir) and Monet (by Renoir) and a photograph of Cézanne setting out to paint from nature at Auvers.

work of his friends, who likewise knew of his and rated it highly. Guillaumin went as far as to declare that Cézanne was a greater painter than Manet. They had in common an independence of mind which rejected the heavy, rigid academic spirit then dominating the Salon. However, for a long time Cézanne took little part in his friends' experiments. His feelings were expressed through dark colours laid on in large swathes, with little importance given to light, and through the use of narrative or allegorical subjects, whereas the others wanted above all to record what they observed.

The first paintings to show that Cézanne had gone over to the new kind of art were the landscapes and still-lifes he did at Auvers-sur-Oise. The grey-greens and browns were still dominant, but no longer laid on in great uniform patches and the compositions were finely structured.

This 'conversion' has generally been attributed to Pissarro, who was

certainly a gifted teacher. He was later to introduce
Gauguin and then Van Gogh (1853–90) to
Impressionism. But his influence does not explain
anything. Why would Cézanne, in the course of a few
months, reject one technique to adopt another when
examples of it had been known to him for several years?
Was it the result of lonely meditation far from his friends
facing the sea at l'Estaque during the winter of 1870–1?
Was it the sudden realization that his own sombre style
had reached a dead-end?

## The first Impressionist exhibition arouses as much hostility as curiosity

In the 19th century, young artists had little opportunity
outside the official Salon to show their work and make
themselves known. Cézanne and his friends were almost
always rejected by the jury of the Salon, which resisted
new ideas.

Claude Monet (1840–1926) then had the courageous
and unusual idea of organizing an independent
exhibition in order to give artists the chance to exhibit
their work in public without the constraints of the Salon.
The exhibition was held from 15 April to 15 May 1874,
a period when Cézanne was already a full member of the
group. Some thirty artists, of varying stature, took part,
but those who led the field were the ones history has

grouped under the name of Impressionists: Edgar Degas, Guillaumin, Monet, Berthe Morisot (1841–95), Pissarro, Renoir, Alfred Sisley (1839–99) and, of course, Cézanne.

The critics made no attempt to understand them. They were put off by the new techniques, so far removed from the over-polished finish of academic painting and by the absence of a subject or anecdote on which to pin a commentary. The painters were either attacked for their lack of intellectual honesty or doubt was cast on their mental stability. Claude Monet was certainly given the worst treatment. He exhibited eight works, one of which was a view of Le Havre harbour entitled *Impression, Sunrise* (1872–3). The title was mocked by the critics, one of whom, Louis Leroy, was responsible for sarcastically inventing the name 'Impressionists' for the group. The artists, however, decided to adopt it.

### 'A sort of idiot who paints in the throes of delirium tremens'

Marc de Montifaud, a woman journalist, did not spare Cézanne. He exhibited three paintings, two of which are fortunately known: *The House of the Hanged Man, Auvers-sur-Oise* (1872–3), *A Modern Olympia* (c. 1873) and a study, *Landscape at Auvers*, which has not been identified for certain.

*The House of the Hanged Man*, one of the very few paintings by Cézanne to be exhibited several

Cézanne, under the tutelage of the 'humble and colossal' Pissarro – as he called the generous master who was always ready to give young artists advice – lightened his palette. At Auvers he met, among others, in 1873 Dr Gachet, an enthusiast of avant-garde painting, who was to look after Van Gogh seventeen years later during the last months of Van Gogh's life. Far left: *The Hermitage at Pontoise* (c. 1867) by Pissarro. Left: Cézanne's *Château of Médan* (c. 1879–81).

In order to put on the first Impressionist exhibition and those that were to follow (there were to be eight in all), the Societé Anonyme des Artistes (Peintres, Sculpteurs, Graveurs etc.), a limited liability company, was formed. Nadar (Félix Tournachon), the famous photographer (1820–1910), lent his former studio at 35 Boulevard des Capucines (photograph left). Pissarro had Cézanne invited to the exhibition in spite of those who feared Cézanne's over-provocative painting. Claude Monet also put in a good word for Cézanne.

times in his life time with his consent, has always been considered the most important canvas he painted in his Impressionist period. The spot chosen, an ordinary village road, the raw light of the Ile-de-France, the use of light silvery colouring even where there was shadow, the summary brushstrokes of a fully loaded brush brought this canvas close to contemporary ones by Monet, Pissarro and Sisley. But what was a search for spontaneity in his friends became for him a conscious yearning for a discipline, and a renunciation of a former style.

*A Modern Olympia* set out either to be a parody or to pay homage to Edouard Manet's famous painting, *Olympia* (1863), which created such a scandal at the Salon of 1865. A recumbent female nude, devoid of a respectable alibi in myth or popular fable, her stark modernity accentuated by the bouquet of flowers, the black servant and the cat, was no more than a prostitute. Cézanne knew Manet and admired him, but, since he was in awe of the elegant Parisian, saw little of him. Cézanne painted two versions of *A Modern Olympia*. In the first (c. 1867) he believed himself to be more modern than Manet in enlarging on what Manet had only suggested. The presence of a gloating client who looks like Cézanne, the still-life, the large blue and gold

In spite of certain characteristics in common, *The House of the Hanged Man* (opposite) of 1872–3 cannot be confused with landscapes by the other Impressionists. The composition is centred around the converging lines radiating from the left and right; the edges of the roofs, of the walls, of the slopes form a series of very precisely connected triangles. The thick, overlaid pigment is plastered on in places with a palette knife.

❛ Don't talk to me about *A Modern Olympia,* there's a good fellow! Alas! just go and see that one. There is a woman bent in two with a black woman lifting the last veil to present her in all her ugliness to a brown puppet. Do you remember Manet's *Olympia*? Well, that was a masterpiece of drawing, of propriety, of finished work compared to M. Cézanne's picture.❜

Louis Leroy
*Le Charivari*
25 April 1874

Top: the second version of *A Modern Olympia* (c. 1873). Left: the first version (c. 1867). Far left: Manet's *Olympia* (1863).

baroque vase with its green plant, the black servant almost reduced to a statue, the heavy curtains – all made a descriptive, anecdotal commentary.

It was the second very different version, painted five or six years later, that was exhibited in 1874. The composition was now balanced, with motifs from the first version being repeated but much modified and generally developed. The green plant became a pot of flowers. The pedestal table and still-life were completed. The black servant statue came to life, the hat on the bed and especially the little dog were outlined with that touch of humour characteristic of the whole work. This painting was one which attracted the most sarcastic

remarks at the exhibition. Marc de Montifaud wrote in *L'Artiste* of May 1874: 'This apparition of a little pink and naked flesh being pushed in an empyrean cloud by a kind of nightmarish demon like a voluptuous vision, this artificial paradise, has suffocated even the strongest-hearted.'

## 'In his works, M. Cézanne is a Greek of the golden age'

In the next few years, Cézanne divided his time between Paris and Aix. Disgusted with the critics, he refused to take part in the group's second exhibition in 1876. However, he was much encouraged by Victor Chocquet, a retired customs official and collector of 18th-century art, who shared his admiration for Delacroix and owned several of his works. Cézanne must certainly have felt reassured to see his own work, as well as Renoir's, which Chocquet was one of the first to admire, placed in a continuing historical perspective by a man of taste. He then decided to participate in the third Impressionist exhibition of 1877. He put in seventeen works and a portrait of Victor Chocquet which particularly attracted the mockery of the critic of *Le Charivari*: 'If you visit the exhibition with a pregnant woman, go quickly past the portrait of a man by M. Cézanne.... This head, the colour of boot-tops, looking so peculiar, could give her a dreadful shock and the infant yellow fever before its birth.'

But this time the Impressionists found a few champions: Louis-Emile-Edmond Duranty,

'Those who have never wielded a paintbrush or a pencil have said he did not know how to draw and they have reproached him for imperfections which are in fact subtle refinements achieved through enormous skill.'

Georges Rivière
*L'Impressioniste*
14 April 1877

In a letter of 11 May 1886 to Victor Chocquet, a keen collector of modern paintings, whose portrait he painted many times (far left), Cézanne expresses respect for him and confesses his attraction to the open air. 'As Delacroix has acted as intermediary between us, I can allow myself to say this: I would have liked to have the intellectual stability which is your hallmark and allows you confidently to achieve whatever goal is proposed.... Chance has not dealt me the same kind of cards.... Otherwise I have no cause for complaint. The sky, the boundless things of nature always enchant me and give me the chance to look at them with pleasure'. Left: *The Pool at the Jas de Bouffan* (c. 1878–9). Above left: Cézanne (c. 1880) and a study for *Three Women Bathers* (c. 1895).

Théodore Duret, a friend of Manet and especially the art critic Georges Rivière, who loudly proclaimed his admiration for Cézanne's works: 'The ignorant people who laugh at *The Bathers*, for example, make me think of barbarians criticizing the Parthenon.'

### Cézanne's output during his Impressionist period includes the same variety of themes as before

Only the literary scenes disappeared. But the spirit in which the same themes were treated was different. People in the countryside no longer appeared in attitudes expressing conflict or indifference but in unison. In certain paintings, most of which could be called men or women bathers, male or more often female nudes are already harmoniously linked with the branches of trees or the lines of the landscape. Cézanne also sometimes contrived great spaces between his figures: he was seeking a rhythm for this theme which he worked at ceaselessly.

### No more skulls or burnt-out candles. Still-lifes bring together life-bearing objects with familiar, simple forms

Flowers and fruit are placed side by side with fruit-dishes, plates, bowls and conical milk cans. Some still-lifes, a genre which the other Impressionists rarely attempted, revealed a new line of research which would become paramount. Cézanne tried to make a clean break with traditional perspective. He did this often in small still-lifes as though he felt more at ease there to experiment. Larger pictures like *Still-life with Soup Tureen* (c. 1877) are more revolutionary in playing with reflections, in rendering mass and colour, than in their 'errors' of perspective.

Cézanne caught the attention of Paul Gauguin at that time: Gauguin was then just an amateur painter who collected Impressionist works. The two painters got to know each other around 1881 through Pissarro.

Gauguin's collection contained canvases by Monet, Renoir and Pissarro which hung side by side with works by Honoré Daumier (1808–79) and Johan Barthold Jongkind (1819–91). He owned three works by Cézanne. One of these, the *Still-life with Compotier* (c. 1880) – precisely one of those where there is distortion of the planes – appears in the background of one of his own paintings: *Portrait of a Woman* (far left below). 'It is the apple of my eye and unless absolutely down to my last shirt, I will hang on to it for dear life,' Gauguin wrote to his friend Emile Schuffenecker in June 1888.

*Still-life with Soup Tureen* (top) is said to have been painted at Pissarro's house in Pontoise around 1877. The light on these humble, rounded objects is rendered by a subtle play of reflections. There are almost no shadows. All this recalls Chardin, ten of whose greatest still-lifes had just been acquired by the Louvre (left: *The Silver Goblet.*) In the *Still-life with Soup Tureen*, the three paintings on the wall give depth to the picture: on the left is a landscape by Pissarro.

## Most of the landscapes combine trees with houses whose walls and roofs allow the introduction of geometric lines

Whether they depicted sites in the vicinity of Paris or in Provence, these landscapes were never based on one single formula. As with the other Impressionists, nature is usually domestic, with the imprint of man, but the human figure is almost always absent.

The viewpoint is often at ground level but at times from above, sometimes a panorama, sometimes narrowly focused. The line of the horizon is seldom in its traditional place (three-fifths of the height); Cézanne mostly puts it very high up. Now rid of the fixed structure plan of the neo-classical landscape taught him by Gibert at Aix, he adopted the formulae of the Barbizon school of painters who did not take much notice of academic rules. Indeed Cézanne always worked on the spot with such precision that the exact place where he had set up his easel could often be identified. His personality had a strong influence on his choice. Cézanne, even more than in the preceding period, started from what lay in front of his eyes, but only in order to interpret it. 'I began to see nature a little late,' he wrote to Zola on 19 December 1878. It was precisely then, during his Impressionist period, that he looked at nature and rendered its changing light with the same fine touch as Monet or Pissarro.

### 'I have begun two little studies with the sea as the subject'

The other Impressionists, at least by 2 July 1876, when Cézanne wrote this to Pissarro, had rarely depicted the sea. Once again Cézanne was different and it was he who suggested in his letter to Pissarro that this time he should follow his lead: 'Your letter surprised me on the sea shore at l'Estaque.... I think the country here would suit you

‘ I am beginning to think myself better than those around me and you must understand that this good opinion I have of myself has only been reached after great deliberation. I have to work all the time, but not so as to arrive at something polished, which is what fools admire. This thing which is so much appreciated by common people is only the result of a workman's craft and makes any resulting painting inartistic and vulgar. I have to try and achieve my vision only for the pleasure of gaining further knowledge and truth.’

Paul Cézanne
Letter to his mother
26 September 1874

Above: *Panoramic View of Auvers* (1873–5). Opposite top right: *Landscape near Médan* (1879–89).

down to the ground.... It's like a playing card. Red roofs against a blue sea.' The essential part played by observation of a static subject – Cézanne worked slowly – was clearly stated, but the comparison with playing cards was of great significance too. At the time, playing cards together with caricature were one of the few kinds of stylized conventions then allowed. This could be called systematic distortion or, in the vocabulary of the time, 'synthesis'. The comparison had already been made for Manet's *Le Fifre*.

Cézanne was searching for subjects that could express his feelings. It is a commonplace in poetry to attribute a 'state of mind' to a landscape. After the French writer Châteaubriand (1768–1848) and the French poet Lamartine (1790–1869), the relationship of man to nature became banal in the 19th century; but examples of visual expression can be found in the past.

Cézanne probably knew Poussin's method (according to which style must be appropriate to the subject matter) or, if he had no knowledge of it, had enough intuition to have discovered its principles standing in front of the magnificent series of forty paintings in the Louvre. It is not the subject alone but the manner of depicting it that distinguishes an heroic landscape from a pastoral one.

° The sun is so terrifying here that it seems as though objects are pared down to silhouettes not only in white or black but in blue, in red, in brown, in violet.... Wouldn't our gentle landscape-painters from Auvers be happy here!°
Paul Cézanne
Letter to Camille Pissarro
L'Estaque, 2 July 1876

Left: *Marseilleveyre and Marie Island* (c. 1882).

## The sky is often reduced to a small light area or else opaque greenery hides it completely

This was the case with two important paintings which formed the beginning and the end of the Impressionist period: *The House of Père Lacroix* (1873) and *The Bridge at Maincy* (1879). The first was painted at Auvers-sur-Oise. The technique is similar to that of *The House of the Hanged Man*. However, while in the latter precise angles of the edges of roofs and walls are clear-cut in the sunlight, the house of *père* Lacroix is buried and hidden in the greenery which casts its shadow over everything.

As for *The Bridge at Maincy*, it has been possible to date it accurately through the discovery of the exact spot. The painting was already famous, but its precise location was not known. A pupil on a school outing recognized the bridge, which featured in a reproduction

*The House of Père Lacroix* (left) is one of the very rare canvases to be signed and dated (1873). Cézanne only signed about twenty and dated about ten of his works, a fact which makes it difficult to establish a precise chronology.

of the painting in his classroom. The bridge that served as a model for Cézanne was thus located at Maincy. Cézanne stayed at Melun from May 1879 to February 1880 and only returned to this region in 1892, when his style was quite different.

This composition of still water enclosed and choked in strangling vegetation is much closer in its wild poetry to the *Château Noir* paintings of c. 1900 than to other landscapes of the period 1878–80. It was one of the few paintings to be copied and sold during the lifetime of the artist. The dark mass of greenery in the *The Bridge at Maincy*, like that in *The House of Père Lacroix*, recalled certain landscapes of the Barbizon school which played its part in the birth of Impressionism.

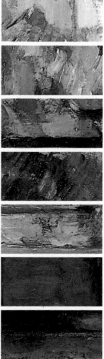

'Cézanne produced his work very slowly and furthermore brought deep thought to bear on it. He never applied a brushstroke which had not been deeply thought out beforehand. He knew what he was doing and what he wanted. He had the secret of presenting our eyes with delicate sensations.'

Emile Bernard
*Souvenirs sur Paul Cézanne*, 1912

## Cézanne paints some twenty portraits in eight years, half of which are self-portraits

Like the other members of the group, Cézanne painted few portraits. The Impressionist technique meant that great attention was paid to surface colour, and so the personality of the model was relegated to second place.

Cézanne often drew the face of his son, Paul, in pencil because he could not make the child stay still in the way he needed a model to do. His son was born on 4 January 1872 without his father's knowledge. Here he is about six or seven years old.

Cézanne did not flatter himself in his self-portraits, even if his expression and pose changed. The choice of unusual hats – cotton turban, haulier's cap, gardener's hat – at a time when wearing a hat was the done thing, underlined the anti-social character Cézanne affected. Cézanne was, as the critic Louis Vauxcelles observed: 'a legendary figure, with a coarse, bristly face'.

In 1878 and 1879 Cézanne made several lengthy stays at Aix and l'Estaque, whereas in previous years he had spent much more time in and around Paris. This withdrawal into himself and search for refuge in l'Estaque was caused by family reasons. It also perhaps helped, by isolating him from the Paris environment, to accelerate a change in his working method. The views of l'Estaque that date from the period 1878–9 have nothing to do with Impressionism.

The critic Louis Vauxcelles described the artist without any malice in *Gil Blas* on 15 September 1904: 'Cézanne is a legendary figure with a coarse, bristly face, his body wrapped in a haulier's rough woollen greatcoat. But this Cézanne is a master.' The painter's self-portraits, representing his head only or half his body, present him without any flattery. He tries to depict physical reality rather than psychological expression. From left to right above: three self-portraits dating from c. 1880, c. 1875 and c. 1877–8 respectively. The last of them once belonged to Pissarro.

'**I** am using all my ingenuity to find my true path in painting,' Cézanne confided to Zola on 24 September 1879. After seven or eight years of using Impressionist techniques, he probably thought he had pushed the analysis of luminous reflections and coloured shadows to the limit. If there was a distinct development around 1880, it was not a totally new departure but a ripening process.

CHAPTER 3
## 'A HARMONY PARALLEL TO NATURE'

**I**n *Flowerpots* (1883–7), the supple stems and the vibration of the light reduce the rigidity of the line of pots. Cézanne explored a completely separate method of expression in watercolour. Few of his French predecessors had given the medium such a central role in their work. Left: *Madame Cézanne in the Garden* (1879–82).

## Cézanne is the first to pass beyond Impressionism but he does not break with it completely

Cézanne remained and would stay faithful to certain principles of this movement, in particular to working outdoors and to coloured shadows. The modification of the colours of an object – whether an apple or a mountain – in terms of the light which illuminated it (one of Impressionism's major discoveries) remained one of the foundations of Cézanne's work in his paintings and watercolours after 1880, and a technique he practised more and more frequently. Indeed, even while working within the Impressionist movement, Cézanne had always kept a sense of form. His compositions, especially his landscapes, were always very carefully constructed.

## The other members of the group also feel the need for renewal

It was perhaps through observing Cézanne's development that the other Impressionists started a strict diet of austerity. Renoir in his own mind called the period when he gave up smothering his shapes in variegated patterns of cotton-wool 'ingresque'. His contours became well-defined and his colours bright and sharp. A little later, Monet painted several large

Cézanne found the peace and quiet he loved at the Jas de Bouffan. He painted its buildings, such as (right) *House and Farm at the Jas de Bouffan* (1885–7), the ornamental lake, the park and its trees throughout the seasons. He made peasants and labourers pose in the garden. After his mother's death, the property was sold in 1899 at his sister's insistence. Before leaving, Cézanne burnt his possessions and personal souvenirs.

The light, thin pigment of *Trees and Houses* (left), dating from 1885 to 1887, as well as the delicate colours call to mind the watercolourist's craft. The composition – a bright open space surrounded by the dark mass of intertwined branches – is one of the most even and symmetrical in all Cézanne's work. Was he casting a glance in the direction of traditional classical landscape taught by his art master Gibert? Opposite below: *Trees and Roof* (c. 1882–3).

canvases where women in bright clothes, sitting in rowing boats, suggested a new concept of space. Pissarro was soon to bow to strict neo-Impressionist disciplines. Cézanne was the first to put everything back into the melting-pot and in a more definitive way, but he was not the only one.

The artist's development did not, however, bring about any cooling of relations with the other members of the group. He stayed more and more often in Aix or l'Estaque, but saw Pissarro again when he returned to Paris. In the spring of 1882 Renoir came to stay at l'Estaque, where Cézanne welcomed him with much kindness. In 1883 Renoir came again, this time in the company of Claude Monet. And during the summer of 1885, Cézanne spent time at Renoir's home at La Roche-Guyon near Paris.

## A technique of square or triangular brushstrokes

In his Impressionist period, Cézanne's impasto was at times thick and gritty, warranting comparison to certain Chardins, and at other times more fluid, put on with long comma-like brushstrokes. After 1880, Cézanne's technique developed. He sometimes placed his touches of paint like square pieces of a mosaic. The pigment remained rather liquid and did not entirely cover the white canvas. In his views of l'Estaque, the abandonment of perspective and flattening of the planes is particularly noticeable. The sea is reduced to a great glossy surface, while the painter uses a full impasto for the rocks.

### 'I paint as I see and as I feel and I have very strong feelings.'

There was an apparent contradiction between Cézanne's profound innovations and his seemingly traditional method of work. The artist never stopped working from nature, whether dealing with still-lifes, people or landscapes. He said he was always on the look-out for beautiful subjects and many critics have laid stress on his lack of imagination and on the so-called 'realist' character of his art. The word can be taken in many ways

'A southern seascape, ponderous blue water, craggy hills, the stupor of things in the heat, strongly composed landscape, all executed with exceptional care and frankness.'

Gustave Geffroy
*Le Journal*
16 February 1894

Above left: *The Gulf of Marseilles Seen from l'Estaque* (c. 1879). Above right: *Bay of L'Estaque* (1879–83). Right: *View of l'Estaque and the Château d'If* (1883–5).

and cause misunderstanding. The creation of a new kind
of spatial structure, which Cézanne only fully developed
after 1895, was the result of obstinate individuality.
Observation of reality was only the point of departure
for subjective painting.

Cézanne often singled out a tree in the foreground of a panoramic landscape. But here in *The Great Pine* (c. 1885) the tree commands all the attention and almost entirely hides the landscape: it is hard to make out a few patches of earth and sky through the brownish network of the branches and the trunk. Cézanne was no longer trying to render the texture of bark, vegetation or land; he was giving unity to his landscape by a uniform treatment of hatched brushstrokes, a little like a watercolour. Thus it is impossible to tell the nature and the distance of the vegetation or parcels of land in the right-hand section, where only the colour is suggested. The choice of the golden section for the intersection of the two strongly indicated principal axes, the vertical and horizontal, again accentuates the monumental character of the work. Without being imposing like the *Mont Sainte-Victoire* series, this painting is imbued with the almost religious spirit Cézanne gave to wild country landscapes.

## It is especially after 1880 that Cézanne's drawing becomes 'heretical' according to the standard practices of the day

Fruit-stands and bottles were no longer truly vertical, the edges of tables no longer protruded from the folds of the drapery partially hiding them, apples were balanced on a chest's sloping lid. It was generally held that a painting represented a fragment of reality (static or moving) as seen by a painter-observer, who was motionless. Manet, Degas and Renoir had discreetly ignored this rule, but in such a way that these dual points of view would only appear as a result of analysis. Cézanne, however, multiplied them in an immediately obvious way. Glasses and fruit dishes are depicted from two or three angles: from the front, from top to bottom and sideways.

This multiplicity of viewpoints would in the course of years be joined by many other 'heresies': disruption of scale, fragmentation of form, dissociation of drawing and colour, introduction of abstract elements to fill out a composition. Cézanne first used still-lifes as a chosen vehicle for his formal experiments, then later extended these 'errors' to the whole of his work.

## For these perfectly harmonious still-lifes Cézanne says he has found 'a good formula'

The still-lifes of the constructive period bear little resemblance to, and do not really derive from, the dark dramatic still-lifes of the early years or the shining, fleshy depiction of objects from the years around 1875. Cézanne assigns to each object and each spot of colour its place in a totally harmonious whole. He had found his own personal style by painting in oils and watercolour. There is no sense of difficulty in these works. In the whole history of painting there are few works more pleasing than some of his still-lifes of the

Most of the objects in *Kitchen Still-life* (below) of 1888–90 are seen from two or three different viewpoints.

• Cézanne's genius is to arrange the whole picture so that the distortion of perspective ceases to be visible in itself when one looks at it as a whole, and only gives the impression, as in normal vision, of a new order being born, of an object in the act of appearing, in the act of coming together in front of our eyes. •
Maurice Merleau-Ponty
*Sens et non-sens*, 1948

1880s. Not only do they satisfy the eye and spirit, but they also reward formal or subject analysis.

## A painter free from influences

This break with the conventions established at the Renaissance led to the invention of a new spatial structure. Cézanne was not the only painter to effect this but he brought it about earlier and went further than anyone else. 'Influences' which might have led him to this step have been sought. In vain. Certainly Cézanne saw examples of art that did not derive from the Italian Renaissance tradition at Aix, in Paris or in the illustrated periodicals proliferating at the time. He could have been inspired by these like Gauguin or Vincent Van Gogh. The abolition of traditional perspective and the third dimension in his painting, as well as the use of planes rising systematically behind objects, are systems of representation of space which are very similar to those in Romanesque fresco or in Japanese prints. However, there is no conclusive evidence whatever to prove that Cézanne was interested in these or that he might have turned his attention in this direction. The range of things in which he was interested, at least as far as it can be specified, was even narrower than Delacroix's, especially if the Middle Ages are considered.

In 1882 the Musée de Sculpture Comparée (later to become the Musée des Monuments Français) opened at the Trocadéro. It exhibited many plaster casts of antique and foreign sculptures comparing them to French ones. Cézanne went there repeatedly. However, he does not seem to have visited the Musée d'Ethnographie, now the Musée de l'Homme, where he might just possibly have seen examples of black and pre-Columbian art.

*The Blue Vase* (1885–7) is one of the most famous canvases of the middle period. Cézanne here creates a strongly defined pictorial space which stands in its own right by the strength of its composition, even if certain objects are charged with symbolic meaning. It is difficult to say if the lines on the right represent a window or part of the wallpaper. Colour also contributes to the unity of the canvas and lights up the shadows to the point where Cézanne can even omit to indicate exactly from where the light is coming.

### *Apples and Biscuits*

One of the simplest still-lifes of Cézanne's mature years, *Apples and Biscuits* (1879–82), best sums up the essential character of his art in his most serene period. In order to create a perfect, consistent composition, a plate and some apples on a chest were enough. The delicacy of the colours in watercolour shades (the pink of the biscuits and the pale blue of the plate), the feigned simplicity of the arrangement, subtly using the space round a few simple objects, is only found in the work of the French painter Lubin Baugin (1610–63) or the Spanish painter Francisco de Zurbarán (1598–1664), though it is unlikely that Cézanne had seen their still-lifes.

## Apples from childhood

Apples have a central place in Cézanne's stylistic experiments. But the fact that he repeatedly chose this fruit had a deeper significance. Above and beyond their traditional erotic symbolism, apples form a part of his early struggles. The young Zola became a childhood friend when the future painter protected the future novelist and Zola gave him apples in gratitude. Cézanne protected him like a big brother (or one could almost say like a father as Zola was an orphan). Cézanne would later paint numerous still-lifes with apples. He wanted, he said, 'to conquer Paris with an apple', in other words to become well-known as a painter of a subject that was at one and the same time both trivial and full of meaning because of tradition and his own childhood memories.

Left: *Still-life on a Table* (1883–7).

On the other hand, he worked at the Louvre all his life. Cézanne's interests led him almost exclusively to classical and baroque sculpture Michelangelo Buonarroti (1475–1564), Pierre Puget (1620–94), the two Coysevox brothers (Antoine Coysevox, French baroque sculptor in the court of Louis XIV and Guillaume Coysevox), Jean-Baptiste Lemoyne (1704–78), Jean-Jacques Caffiéri (1725–92), though also to antique sculpture and at rare moments to the Middle Ages.

His field of interest was wider in painting, but the artists he studied most were Rubens (1577–1640) and Delacroix. Altogether, nearly one third of the drawings preserved by Cézanne (there are very few copies in oil) were copies of works of art.

**Cézanne's father intercepts a letter from Chocquet to his son. He discovers that his son is living with an artist's model and that he has a child**

In 1878 Cézanne came to l'Estaque again looking for a refuge for Hortense Fiquet and their son Paul. He wanted to hide this liaison from his father, and so he had to come back home every evening. When his father discovered the truth, the artist denied that he was having an affair, but Louis-Auguste reduced Cézanne's allowance. For several months Cézanne was obliged to call on the generosity of Zola, who was in funds because of his success as an author.

Relations became strained. Louis-Auguste pretended not to know what he did in fact know: 'It seems I have grandchildren in Paris.' The painter found an ally in his mother and, though this is less certain, in his sister Marie. Neither much liked Hortense, from whom Paul was anyway gradually breaking away. They joined forces, however, in 1885 to brush aside a certain Fanny with whom the painter started an affair, though little is known about it.

Paul finally married Hortense in 1886 under pressure from his family. He was forty-seven years old and his son was fourteen. Louis-Auguste gave his consent to the marriage, but died a few months after the ceremony.

Cézanne felt an affinity with the dramatic genius of the southern sculptor, Pierre Puget, and made several drawings from his works like this *Milo of Crotona* (1882–5).

### Emile Zola, his life-long friend, does not understand Cézanne's talent any more than Cézanne's father did

It was also in 1886 that the row between Cézanne and Zola occurred. Cézanne had often asked favours of Zola, who had very willingly helped. For Cézanne, Zola was a mixture of people: the childhood friend, the young critic of the Café Guerbois championing the new painting in Manet's circle, the successful writer who for a time stood in for his father when he failed to come up with his allowance, and the friend on whom he relied to recognize the worth of his painting. Zola certainly defended Manet in 1867, but he seems to have understood and appreciated the Impressionists' or Cézanne's art only for the modernity of the subject matter, not for anything else. As the years went by, his articles on the Impressionists became more and more reserved. There is evidence of this in a letter from the writer and critic Joris-Karl Huysmans to Pissarro in 1883. 'I have taken to Cézanne strongly, for through Zola I know of his efforts, his disappointments, his failures when he tries to launch a work of art.' Moreover, Zola's very aesthetics, his taste for heavy and pretentious furniture, the fact he had taken down his friends' pictures from his walls, except for Manet's portrait, all confirmed where his choice lay.

Even when their relations were difficult, Cézanne always showed deference to his father (below). His parents did not attend the religious wedding ceremony for his marriage to Hortense Fiquet at the Church of

Saint-Jean-Baptiste at Aix-en-Provence on 29 April 1886, but they were present at the civil ceremony the day before and they signed the marriage register at the town hall in Aix.

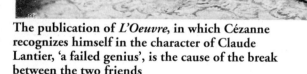

**The publication of *L'Oeuvre*, in which Cézanne recognizes himself in the character of Claude Lantier, 'a failed genius', is the cause of the break between the two friends**

In 1886 Zola, as he always did on the publication of one of his new novels, sent a copy of *L'Oeuvre* to Cézanne. Zola's supporters said he never wanted to feature his friend in it. However, his contemporaries recognized Cézanne in the portrait of this feeble painter.

If Zola's portrayal of Cézanne was unintentional, it makes it all the more revealing. For Zola around 1885, Cézanne was a failed artist and an embarrassing friend. It has to be said also that at Médan Cézanne had behaved very inconsiderately to the writer, treating him in an off-hand way in front of his guests.

On 4 April 1886 Cézanne wrote a very curt letter of thanks to Zola that put an end to a long friendship, though with much dignity. The two men were never to see each other again.

## During the constructive period, Cézanne paints l'Estaque and its vicinity over twenty times

The painter described his house in a letter to Zola of 24 May 1883: 'I have a little house and garden here just above the station at the foot of the hill where the rocks and pines begin to rise behind me. I am always busy with

my painting, I have some fine viewpoints here.' Usually he brought sea, mountains, houses, greenery together and occasionally – an unusual detail which he was without doubt one of the first to dare paint – a factory chimney. The sea is reduced to a kind of lifeless, motionless blue sheet. This reduction of the sea to a flat plane contrasts strongly with the surrounding greenery and houses, which Cézanne readily cuts up into geometric shapes. In the canvases painted during his early stays, the vegetation is most often thick and bushy, combining the most varied hues of green and yellow. Later the representation of the site is the main consideration. The artist even attracted Renoir to l'Estaque. Renoir had never worked in the Midi before and was equally taken by 'this beautiful country'.

**'** My dear Emile, I have just received *L'Oeuvre*, which you were good enough to send me. I thank the author of *Les Rougon-Macquart* for this kind token of remembrance and ask him to allow me to shake him by the hand in memory of years gone by. Ever yours moved by the feeling of past times. **'**
Paul Cézanne
Letter to Emile Zola
Gardanne, 4 April 1886

Monet also wrote to Zola (depicted opposite far left in his study at Médan in a photograph of c. 1897) from Giverny on 5 April 1886: 'I have just read *L'Oeuvre*, and I confess it has left me troubled and uneasy...I am afraid that just as we are about to succeed, our enemies will make use of your book to bludgeon us.'

Cézanne helped succeeding generations to discover Mediterranean light. Before him, artists had been especially familiar with the Normandy coast. Cézanne had Monet and Renoir to stay and it was at l'Estaque that Georges Braque (1882–1963) and Raoul Dufy (1877–1953) were to paint most like Cézanne. Above: *The Gulf of Marseilles Seen from l'Estaque* (1883–5). Left: *Self-portrait* (1880).

Cézanne practically never represented the sea except at l'Estaque (left). A psychoanalyst would readily note the connection *mer-mère-refuge* to be seen in Cézanne's sojourns on the Mediterranean shore. Later Cézanne had to leave l'Estaque for several reasons. One of these had to do with the increasing industrialization of the place. Cézanne pointed it out to his niece in a letter of 1 September 1902 which revealed his state of mind: 'I remember the shore at l'Estaque perfectly and it was so picturesque. Unfortunately what is called progress is nothing but an invasion of bipeds who never stop until they have transformed everything into hideous quays with gas lamps and – what is worse – with electric lighting. What a time we are living in!'

## Trees and buildings are etched with distinct contours on the canvas in the landscapes

In the 1920s, after Cubism, many critics of Cézanne dwelt on the geometric lines in the form of grids to which his paintings could be reduced. Certainly the rectilinear sharp edges of the Jas de Bouffan or the staggered tiers of roofs at Gardanne near Aix lend themselves to this kind of interpretation. It was in 1885 and 1886 that Cézanne found a source of inspiration there, as he describes in a letter to Zola of 25 August 1885: 'I am beginning to paint at last because I have almost no worries. I go to Gardanne every day and I come back every evening to the country, to Aix.' Cézanne here speaks revealingly of the two conditions necessary before he could create a work of art: tranquillity of mind and a stimulating scene.

The contours of trees and houses in his Impressionist period were swathed in or shaken by a kind of vibration. After 1880 the light in Cézanne's landscapes changed completely. For the most part there is a hard uniform light outlining shapes which, unlike Impressionist light, is not analysed in a systematic way. It is impossible to tell the time of day or the season of the year.

Compared to Monet's or Sisley's poplars, shimmering in the sun, Cézanne's have the solidity and immobility of bronze. This luminosity, this improbable positioning of shadows, is especially marked in the majestic landscapes dating from 1885 to 1890. Here Cézanne achieved the same poetic serenity as in Poussin's heroic landscapes. Right: Cézanne's *Poplars* (1879–82). Below, from left to right: details of Monet's *Poplars* (1891), Sisley's *Moret, Beside the Loing* (1892), Cézanne's *Poplars*, and in vignette, Monet's and Sisley's complete pictures.

## Cézanne starts work on the Mont Sainte-Victoire series, the most famous and the richest of them all

In a letter of May 1881 Cézanne told Zola: 'I have begun several studies [of the same subject], some in overcast weather, some in full sunlight.' Some ten years later Monet adopted this working method with his series on *Haystacks* ( 1890–1), *Poplars* (1891), *Rouen Cathedral* (1892–4), his views of the Thames in London (1900–4) and finally, from the beginning of the century, *The Waterlilies*. Cézanne was thus one step ahead of Monet.

The Mont Sainte-Victoire appeared for the first few times in 1870, then as a picture within a picture in *The Eternal Feminine*, also known as *The Triumph of Women* (c. 1877). However, it was only after 1880 that Cézanne became so passionately obsessed with 'his' mountain.

Before 1890 it was usually in the background of a very structured landscape with tiers of planes, depth being suggested by a tree in the foreground and by successive horizontal and oblique lines. The light is clear and even; the atmosphere limpid. As in his humble still-lifes, Cézanne presents an image of a world at peace in his imposing panoramas.

## The Mont Sainte-Victoire symbolizes the painter dominating his surroundings

Sites in the vicinity of Aix had often been an inspiration for Cézanne, but rarely in a panoramic view. The Mont Sainte-Victoire, which dominates the countryside round Aix, its colours changing hour by hour, made its appearance just as Cézanne came to spend less and less time in Paris and much more in Aix. His relations with his father had gradually become much more relaxed. He no longer had money worries and had finally legalized his situation by marrying Hortense Fiquet.

The serenity of these landscapes can be seen as a reflection of the new calm in his family life, and the dominating position of the mountain as the symbol of Cézanne himself taking possession of his territory and triumphing over the people of Aix, who did not want to recognize his artistic talent. In the 19th century Aix-en-Provence was a sleepy little town with a population of

The Mont Sainte-Victoire belongs to the family of 'sacred' mountains: Sinai, Tabor, Olympus. Its name, whose origins are controversial, gives it a domineering and venerable image.

30,000 inhabitants. In the Middle Ages it was the old capital of Provence, but it was usurped by its rival Marseilles and had only kept the court of appeal, the archbishop's palace and the university as a mark of its former position. As a student Cézanne had suffered the dreary life of Aix; as a painter he bitterly felt his fellow-citizens' lack of understanding. Even so, its provincial calm was probably not unpleasing to the solitary genius.

This *Mont Sainte-Victoire* was painted around 1885. A lone pine in the centre of the composition is a bold, unorthodox way of giving depth to the landscape.

‘ You see the mountain well before Le Tholonet. It is bare and almost monochrome, more a flash of light than a colour. Sometimes the shape of the clouds can be confused with high mountains: here it is quite the reverse; the dazzling mountain at first sight seems to have emerged from the sky. This impression is reinforced by the movement of the rocky flanks falling in parallel folds as though petrified in an age before time or extending horizontally at the base of the mountain. The mountain seems to have flowed from on high, from the almost identically coloured sky, and to have thickened here into a little massif from universal space.’

Peter Handke
*Die Lehre der Sainte-Victoire*, 1980

Opposite above: *Mont Sainte-Victoire* (1882–5). Opposite below: *Mont Sainte-Victoire* (1885–7). Left: photograph from the beginning of the century of the road from Le Tholonet to the Mont Sainte-Victoire.

## Madame Cézanne and young Paul

There are many pictures of Madame Cézanne in the last decade of the 19th century. The features of her face are sometimes vague and inexpressive or else the expression is solemn and thoughtful. Certain strongly structured

The portraits of Madame Cézanne, with their clear, simplified volumes, particularly interested the Cubist painters.

portraits of her also date from the end of this classic period, as well as *Woman with a Coffee-pot* (1890–5), where the body and objects are simplified into geometric lines. The model for this canvas is not known. It was

thought to be Madame Brémond, the painter's housekeeper. After 1880, young Paul's face appeared in a few pictures. Cézanne's son was very fond of his father. He was to write to him often and was an emotional help for him at the end of his life.

In 1888, Paul Cézanne sat for a big composition called *Mardi Gras*, inspired by the traditional carnival at Aix-en-Provence.

Mardi Gras (top) is one of the very few paintings after 1870 to include figures in movement. Above centre: studies for *Mardi Gras* (c. 1888). Above: *Louis Guillaume in Pierrot Costume* (1888). Opposite: *Madame Cézanne in the Conservatory* (1891–2), the famous portrait of Hortense, whose grace and elegance is enhanced by its unfinished state. Left: *Woman with a Coffee-Pot* (1890–5).

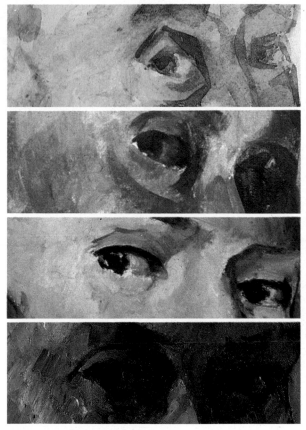

Cézanne's self-portraits are surely the most lively, the most spontaneous, of all his portraits and have the fewest props. Opposite top: *Self-portrait* (c. 1895). Opposite below, from left to right: *Self-portrait in a Soft Hat* (1890–4); *Self-portrait in a Bowler Hat* (1883–5); *Self-portrait* (1879–82), which once belonged to Degas. This page: details of Cézanne's eyes in these self-portraits.

'Cézanne has the talent to show the essential part of a person. The eye, reddened through having questioned the imponderable for too long, understood how to reveal the inner life under the iridescent skin.'

André Lhote
'Cézanne ou la lenteur'
*La nouvelle Revue française*
1 April 1939

## To paint his own portrait, Cézanne chooses a new pose: bust in profile

The painter's head turns left towards the person looking at him. The choice of a sudden movement introduced a new element in the series of self-portraits. In another painting, *Self-portrait with Palette* (c. 1890), Cézanne conforms to the traditional position of the painter without giving up his bold innovations in perspective, and depicts himself standing in front of his easel, palette in hand. He holds his palette rather awkwardly in his right hand.

## *The Bathers* series comes to maturity

Compared to his academic or revolutionary contemporaries, Cézanne's output was striking in the richness and diversity of its themes. Certain genres, however, seemed to go through a period of slow ripening rather than sudden fruition. This is so with the theme of the bathers. He painted many of these pictures of modest size, which were to reach their conclusion later. The fact that they were experimental works perhaps explains why many artists (Claude Monet, Maurice Denis, Henri Matisse, Pablo Picasso and Henry Moore) wanted to own an example from this series. However, they must not be seen merely as experimental works or unfinished trial sketches. The very variable number of figures and the diversity of the poses only prove that Cézanne had not yet found an arrangement that satisfied him. Many versions at the end of the classic period with clearly distributed masses, the blue-toned, almost Impressionist brightness of his nudes, and their enamel-like technique, cannot be considered as experimental paintings.

● With Cézanne male and female bathers are not weighed down with any historical or mythological role, nor clothed in any fiction: they are shown in all their naked truth. Neither do they have this anecdotal side which makes the Impressionists on the banks of the Marne with their graceful reportage so entrancing.●

Gilles Plazy
*Cézanne ou la Peinture absolue*, 1988

Opposite top: *Five Bathers* (1879–92), once belonged to Picasso. Opposite bottom: *Three Bathers* (1887–90). Below: *Male Bathers* (1890–4).

Cézanne had followed a difficult road, guided only by his inner convictions. He had overcome much opposition and his art had opened up a new path in painting. However, in January 1903 he confessed modestly to the art dealer Ambroise Vollard: 'I have made some progress. Why so late and with such difficulty? Is art indeed a priesthood which claims the pure in heart and takes them over completely?'

CHAPTER 4

## 'I BEGIN TO SEE THE PROMISED LAND'

Whether a still-life, figure or landscape, all motifs are treated with spirit and freedom. Opposite: *Vallier Seated* (c. 1906). Below: *Still-life: Apples, Pears and Pot* (*The Kitchen Table*) (1900–4).

## The death of his father makes Cézanne rich, but he continues to lead a very simple life in Aix

After 1890 the painter's existence was more widely known; we learn more about him from visitors. It is easy to think that he would have seized the opportunity, being well off, to travel to Italy or Belgium to see other works by the masters he had admired in the Louvre, or, like Monet and Degas, to form a collection. Nothing of the kind; Cézanne kept to his very simple lifestyle. Apart from taking the waters at Vichy (he suffered from diabetes) and making a visit to Switzerland in 1890, at the behest of his wife – 'she only likes Switzerland and lemonade,' he said – he hardly left his favourite places: Aix and its surrounding region, with a few, increasingly brief, trips to Paris and its surroundings.

At Aix, he lived closer to his sister than his wife and even ended up by taking a housekeeper. He led a regular life, became a practising Christian and was a diligent worshipper at the cathedral. He painted almost every day, being driven by carriage to work on the spot, or painting at home. In 1902 he set up a new studio on the road to Les Lauves, in the immediate vicinity of Aix, from which he overlooked the town and had a good viewpoint on to the Mont Sainte-Victoire.

## In November 1895 Ambroise Vollard organizes in Paris the first exhibition of Cézanne's work, which is still unknown to the public

Cézanne had, however, shown a few canvases in group exhibitions. But the shop of *père* Tanguy, an enterprising colour merchant in Montmartre who took paintings in pawn, was the only place they could be seen.

The painter Maurice Denis (1870–1943), who executed a solemn *Homage to Cézanne* (see p. 151) in 1900, admitted that towards 1890, at around the time of his first visits to Tanguy's shop, he took Cézanne to be a myth, perhaps even the pseudonym of an artist engaged in other research but whose existence he doubted.

It was certainly at *père* Tanguy's that Ambroise Vollard (a young Creole recently established as an art dealer) also saw some paintings by Cézanne for the first time. Gifted

• Vollard poses every morning at Cézanne's and has done so for an age. Whenever he moves, Cézanne complains that he makes him lose his train of thought. He also talks about his own lack of optical qualities, and of his inability to realize his vision like the old masters; but he believes himself to have feelings,• wrote the painter Maurice Denis in his diary. Ambroise Vollard was to say in 1914: 'It is difficult for anyone who has not seen him paint to realize just how slow and laborious his work was on certain days.' After one hundred and fifteen sittings – again according to Vollard – the painter went back to Aix. Above: photograph of the Trois-Sautets bridge in the vicinity of the town c. 1900.

**Exposition Cézanne**
Galerie Vollard
6, Rue Laffitte

Composition inédite de Cézanne          du lundi 9 mai au vendredi 10 juin 1898

with exceptional flair, the young novice dealer organized the first exhibition of Cézanne's work. From then Vollard applied himself to making his protégé's work known (Cézanne was to do his portrait) and he bought the major part of the artist's output.

In 1895 two paintings, *Farmyard at Auvers* (c. 1879), see p. 158, and *The Gulf of Marseilles Seen from L'Estaque* (c. 1879), see p. 66, entered the Luxembourg museum, after difficult negotiations, as part of the paintings in the bequest of the painter Gustave Caillebotte (1848–94). He had been a generous supporter of the Impressionists and admired Cézanne, as did Monet, Degas, Renoir and Gauguin.

**Young painters revere Cézanne; painters and critics write about him; some go to see him at Aix**

In spite of his reputation for unsociability and his phobia

Cézanne painted the *Portrait of Ambroise Vollard* four years after the exhibition in Vollard's gallery in 1895.

about the slightest physical contact, Cézanne received the newcomers amiably and kept up an open correspondence with some of them. This was the case with Charles Camoin (b. 1879), the future Fauve, and Emile Bernard (1868–1941), Gauguin's rival in the invention of the Cloisonnist style, who had by then, however, returned to a more traditional method. It was in a letter to Bernard of 15 April 1904 that Cézanne wrote the by-now famous sentence: 'Treat nature by means of the cylinder, the sphere, the cone, with everything in proper perspective so that each side of an object or plane is directed towards a central point. Lines parallel to the horizon give breadth, that is a section of nature, or, if you prefer, of the spectacle which the *pater omnipotens aeterne deus* spreads before our eyes. Lines perpendicular to this horizon give depth.'

The importance of this sentence, which appeared to contain the seeds of Cubism and constitute a watershed in 20th-century painting, has probably been exaggerated. Cézanne had a tendency, because of his good nature, to adapt his written or spoken answers to his audience.

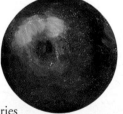

He considered Bernard to be, as he put it in a letter to his son of 26 September 1906, 'an intellectual saturated with memories

Objects with simple shapes like fruit or bottles were often placed near drapery, which introduced suppleness and movement into the still-life composition. Above, left and below: details of *Still-life with Onions* (c. 1895). Below: detail of *Apples and Oranges* (c. 1895–1900).

from museums'. And it must be said that Cézanne, a little mischievously, had learnedly formulated a theory that simplified everything for him.

### Certain compositions like *The Cardplayers* reach their final form

*The Cardplayers* is one of Cézanne's most popular works. The subject was present in painting from the 17th century, and a picture by the

Le Nain brothers on this theme is kept in the Musée Granet in Aix. There are five versions of *The Cardplayers*, plus some preparatory studies for isolated figures: one version with five characters, one with four and three with two. There has been lengthy discussion on the order in which these five versions were painted. It seems that for stylistic reasons the three versions with two characters are later than the others where the composition is less concentrated and where the characters stand out against a light background. All the versions are based on a highly symmetrical arrangement; the central axis is marked in the earliest two by a person facing the spectator and in the other three by a bottle.

Why did Cézanne decide to give so much attention to the theme of cardplayers just as he was painting a series of *The Bathers*? *The Cardplayers*, with their concentrated appearance, facing each other in a closed space, are the direct antithesis of *The Bathers* with their impersonal silhouettes elaborated in an open-air setting. Above: *The Cardplayers* (1890–2) in the Barnes Foundation in Philadelphia, one of the largest of Cézanne's compositions (134 cm by 181 cm) gives a strong impression of concentration and tension. Left: the much more serene *Cardplayers* (1890–2) in the Metropolitan Museum of New York. In this painting the confrontation is more restrained.

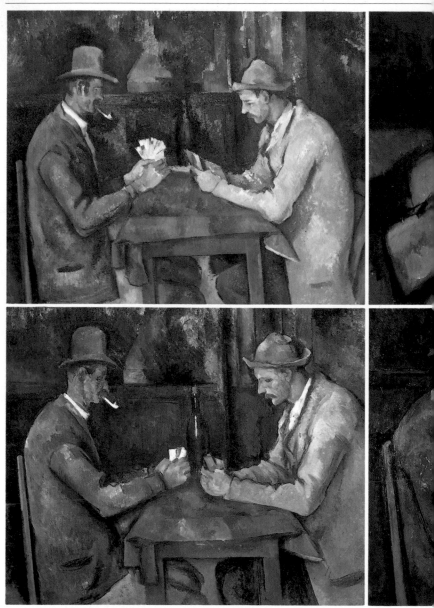

Did Cézanne in this series unconsciously express the struggle that he had had to wage with his father and also with himself? The playing card symbolizes both a weapon and his work as a painter. In the art-critics' vocabulary of the period, in one of Cézanne's own letters (1876) and in discussions around the table at the Café Guerbois, it was used to symbolize the simplified style and flattened drawing of Manet and the Impressionists. These three versions of *The Cardplayers* – from 1890–5 (opposite top and bottom) and 1890–2 (left bottom and detail top) – reduce the composition to a duel between the two antagonists. They all express extreme tension between the two characters concentrating on their game. The setting has virtually entirely disappeared. The technique is very free, the colour being applied in determined brushstrokes.

## At the risk of upsetting his admirers, Cézanne makes a completely fresh start in his work for the third time

He did this at a time when his earlier works were beginning to be known and liked, at least by a small nucleus of admirers. His new technique was in no way a logical progression from his earlier work. It is, quite possibly, a unique case in the history of painting.

The subject matter is just as rich as ever: portraits, still-lifes, landscapes, figures. But between 1890 and 1895 a radical change of style and treatment took place. Following those serene arrangements with occupied space and voids, there came a succession of opaque compositions, and, after light and luminous tones, dark browns and dark blues.

From now on, traditional perspective and modelling by shadow were totally abandoned. At times, space does not really exist any more and all the elements constituting the picture are placed on a single continuous plane without depth: this is the case with the *Forest* (see p. 106) and *Women Bathers* canvases and with certain *Mont Sainte-Victoire* paintings. At other times Cézanne defines a new kind of spatial structure by an arrangement of planes at an oblique angle to the picture plane.

## Once again, it is in still-life that his new experiments are most clearly expressed

From now on, more sure of himself than he would admit in his letters, he chose canvases of quite a large size. His

Left: *Apples and Oranges* (c. 1895–1900). Below: *Still-life with Onions* (c. 1895). Opposite: *Still-life with a Plaster Cupid* (c. 1895).

compositions were more complex. The simple forms and the polished surfaces of apples and crockery contrast strongly with the moving, irregular folds of the drapery in both *Apples and Oranges* and *Still-life with Onions*. The description of objects and the arrangement of planes defy all laws and form a coherent world where each touch of colour is determined by its place in the whole. Cézanne introduced a plaster statuette, a plump and dimpled 17th-century Cupid – formerly attributed to Pierre Puget (1620–94), but now believed to be by François Duquesnoy (1595–1643) – in the midst of the fruit and drapery in *Still-life with a Plaster Cupid*. The apples and the statuette are evocative images with a symbolic value.

Cézanne is once again using the dark colours of his youth. At the same time he paints large watercolours like *Skull on a Drapery* (left) of 1902–6, playing with the effects of transparency. There is the same freedom in the composition of his still-lifes, in which he never hesitates, contrary to common practice, to place objects out of balance.

The chubby cherub clearly stands for health, youth and *joie de vivre*. In contrast, Cézanne returned at the end of his life to the skull motif, which had disappeared from his work since the end of the 1860s.

### Portraits and individual figures both undergo drastic simplification

There were still just as many portraits of his wife. He changed her pose and the setting, making her sit in the open air or in a conservatory. Madame Cézanne almost always appeared distant, majestic, and was placed purposely by the painter in a rather constrained attitude and in an indeterminate light.

By its emphasis on naturalness and by the importance given to the model's surroundings and profession, the painting of Gustave Geffroy belongs to the humanist portrait tradition. Geffroy was an art critic who was very close to Monet, and the latter called his attention to Cézanne in 1894. He published two articles favourable to Cézanne, who was then still almost unknown. Cézanne painted his portrait in order to thank him. The two men were to fall out in the end. Geffroy certainly had not shown great understanding of either the painter's art or his personality.

Relations between Cézanne and Joachim Gasquet were to follow a similar course. This young poet from Aix, the son of one of Cézanne's childhood friends, took a liking to him and

Geffroy thought Cézanne's portrait of him (below) of 1895 one of the painter's finest works, in spite of its unfinished state: 'The library, the papers on the table, the little plaster copy of a Rodin, the artificial rose he brought at the beginning of the sittings, all is outstanding work. Moreover, there is actually a person too in this setting, painted with scrupulous care and a richness of tones and a harmony that are incomparable.'

became enthusiastic about the painter's art. Cézanne took him into his confidence for a time. Their relations were to become strained because Gasquet was indiscreet and because Cézanne, touchy and unsociable, was always afraid of 'falling into someone's clutches'. Gasquet published the transcript of his conversations

In the *Portrait of Joachim Gasquet* (below) and *Man with Folded Arms* (opposite top) there are strong distortions of the planes.

Images of encroaching vegetation, where the eye is lost, are found in Gauguin, Monet and in the *Jungles* of Henri 'le Douanier' Rousseau (1844–1910). They contrast strongly with the open panoramas and large skies of which Cézanne and the Impressionists had been fond during the 1870s. Left: *Forest* (1895–1900).

with the artist, adding much of his own invention. Cézanne commemorated their friendship with a portrait.

### In the landscapes the eye comes up against a wall of lush vegetation surrounding gigantic rocks

In the period before, Cézanne's landscapes were organized around an open horizon and tiers of planes. This taste for a wilderness without horizons, from which man was excluded, like that of Bibémus quarry, was shared by Claude Monet in his great *Waterlilies*. The forest is treated with a delicate technique, each brushstroke being posed with a watercolourist's lightness and sureness of hand, and there are very few corrections. Like Poussin, Cézanne changed his technique to differentiate between substances. The impasto is smooth for the rocks, broken up for the foliage, with at times a light trembling movement to suggest the wind in the trees. In the outstanding *Lake Annecy*, the whole of the canvas becomes a wall of blue-toned ice. Few painters have known how to vary their medium to this extent.

Cézanne painted *Château Noir* at least ten times, seen from above and below or else frontally in a plane parallel to that of the picture. He produced a striking effect through the contrast of the ochre building and the streaks of the deep-green foliage in the sky.

The Mont Sainte-Victoire continued to inspire him, but the viewpoints and the setting had changed. He often set up his easel on the road to Le Tholonet and painted it face on.

> ❛ Here I am, far from our Provence for a little.... This is a temperate zone. The height of the surrounding hills is quite considerable. The lake, constricted here by two gulleys, seems to lend itself to young misses' drawing exercises. It is certainly nature still, but a little like we have been taught to see it in young women travellers' albums of paintings. ❜
>
> Paul Cézanne
> Letter to Joachim Gasquet
> Annecy, July 1896

> ❛ I am doing some painting to stop being bored. It isn't very amusing, but the lake is very fine with big hills all around, they say two thousand metres, but it isn't a patch on our part of the world. ❜
>
> Paul Cézanne
> Letter to Emile Solari
> Annecy, July 1896

Left: *Lake Annecy* (1896).

## Château Noir

• Situated halfway between Aix and the village of Le Tholonet, Château Noir had been built in the second half of the 19th century somewhat above the road near the bottom of the wooded hill that rises behind it. It consists of two separate buildings, set at a right angle to each other...A series of pillars...rise into the sky, supporting nothing, and lend the complex an incongruous aspect of ruins. Incongruous, too, is the style of the buildings, with their narrow Gothic windows and steep roofs. Between them lies the court that Cézanne's room overlooks...Even the name...'Château Noir' is a misnomer, for there is nothing black about it, nor is it a château; it is built of the beautiful yellow stone from the nearby Bibémus quarry...In Cézanne's paintings it is always the glow of the orange-gold façade of the west wing, livened by the large red barn door...that dominates the unruly blue-green vegetation. •

John Rewald
'The Last Motifs at Aix'
*Cézanne: The Late Work*
Ed. by William Rubin
The Museum of Modern
Art, New York, 1978

### Green and ochre harmonies

' The sensations of colour which give the light cause abstractions which do not allow me to cover my canvas, nor to complete the limits of objects where their points of contact are fine and delicate; hence it follows that my image or picture is incomplete. '
Paul Cézanne
Letter to Emile Bernard
23 October 1905

Opposite: *In the Park at Château Noir* (c. 1898). Above: *Pistachio Tree in the Courtyard of Château Noir* (c. 1900). Above left: *Château Noir* (1894–6). Left: detail of *Château Noir* (1904–6).

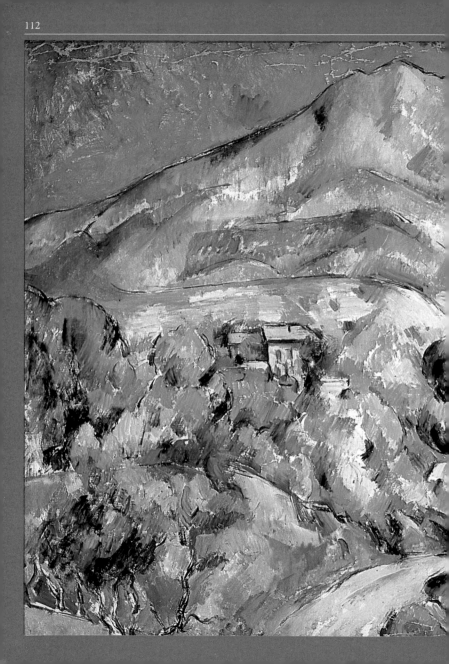

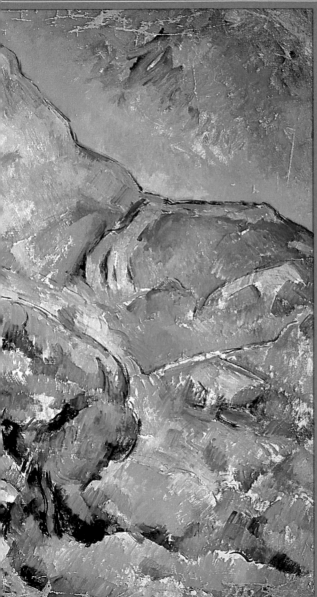

## The triumphant mountain

In *Mont Sainte-Victoire above the Road of Le Tholonet* (left and detail overleaf) of 1896–8, the mountain remains integrated within the panorama; there is no break, no rift between the plain and the low hills on the one hand and the mountain on the other. The colours are disposed simply but rendered naturalistically in spirit: the sky is blue, the vegetation green, the earth light ochre and the mountain pink-blue. The shift from one plane of colour to another follows sinuous, irregular contour lines with few transitional spaces. Joachim Gasquet gave evidence about Cézanne finishing one of these *Sainte-Victoire* paintings: 'The canvas slowly acquired a sense of equilibrium. The preconceived image, well thought-out and linear, was already emerging from the patches of colour defining it on all sides. The landscape seemed to flicker, for Cézanne had slowly worked round each object, taking samples, as it were, of each colour; day by day, imperceptibly, he had brought together all these values into sure harmony, linking them together with a muted kind of clarity.'

## 'To marry the curves of women to the rumps of the hills'

During his last years Cézanne set to work on an important canvas on the theme of women bathers; he even let himself be photographed by Emile Bernard sitting in front of it. This subject had always interested him, but he had hitherto confined himself to quite small-sized canvases. Around 1900, for the first time, he began to tackle pictures more than a metre wide. The largest version (see pp. 120–1) measured 2.08 m by 2.49 m; it was much the biggest of Cézanne's paintings. He had an opening made in the wall of his studio on the Chemin des Lauves so that it could go in without being rolled.

Cézanne painted at least three large versions of the *Great Bathers*. The number and position of the figures vary markedly from one to another: two frieze-like versions, which are striking and powerful and without parallel in the other canvases of the period were worked on for a long time, put aside and then undertaken again. It is thought one was in the Paris studio and the other at Aix and that he worked alternately on one and then the other. The faces give an unfinished impression reinforced by lack of development in height. The third, the largest, is composed as a superb gothic arch, while the other two are more like bas-reliefs. The colouring in the largest picture has the delicacy of a watercolour, with dominant blue-greys. Once more Cézanne had expressed ideal harmony in the satisfying union between the figures and the natural surroundings.

Once more he is on a level with Poussin's most poetic humanist creations, in which he recognized a powerful lyricism held in check. A remark of Cézanne about Poussin is often incorrectly quoted. He stated that he wished 'to imbue Poussin with life by contact with nature' ('vivifier Poussin sur nature') (and not 'remake [refaire] Poussin according to nature'), that is, to embody the emotion he experienced in the face of nature within the discipline of a Poussin landscape. He left us landscapes which have both grandeur and order, into which people fit harmoniously.

## Women, trees and sky

' Rather than a study for [the *Great Bathers* (1900–6)], this seems to be an independent version in which...the figures are no longer the primary focus, at least not as they appear in this unfinished work. But it is 'unfinished' merely because there are spots of canvas left uncovered; these occur in places where only colors – not compositional elements – are missing...This loosely brushed picture is completely dominated by blue gray tonalities with a few greenish blue tints in the ground, the trees and the sky.... The darkest spot of the composition is a deep blue triangle in the center foreground, around which four nudes are gathered. Their group is separated from those at the left and right in an arrangement not found elsewhere in Cézanne's work, except in a watercolor. Most of the bare white spaces are concentrated around the groups of bathers on either side of this center. The figures of the central group appear to be bending down, as though their attention were attracted by something on the ground.'
John Rewald
*Cézanne: The Late Work*
Ed. by William Rubin
1978

### Great Bathers

❛ It is the largest of
Cézanne's pictures and
because it is also the
most formal in aspect,
it has been cited often
as an example of his
ideal of composition...It
is exceptional among his
work, however, in the
marked symmetry and
the adaptation of the
nude forms to the
triangular pattern of
the trees and the
river...The atmosphere
of this painting is
strange and beautiful –
the landscape is largely
bluish, a soft haze in
which sky and water and
vegetation merge and by
which the masterfully
drawn figures are
delicately overcast.❜
Meyer Schapiro
*Cézanne*, 1988

### Cézanne's very last works display freedom and a visionary character

Already in *Boy with a Red Waistcoat* and in *The Cardplayers* Cézanne hardly bothered with exact anatomical details and lengthened his models' arms outrageously.

The *Old Woman with a Rosary* (1895–6) or the different versions of the gardener Vallier have a compassionate side which had disappeared from his world for over twenty years. Dark colours (Prussian blue, dark green, brown), thick impasto and the tragic expression of the faces marked by age, all separate these moving figures from those of the preceding period.

He despaired of being able to render 'this magnificent richness of colouring which animates nature'. On 8 September 1906 he wrote to his son: 'Here on the banks of the river there are so many subjects and the same one seen from a different angle makes a powerful and

This serious, pensive face of the *Boy with a Red Waistcoat* (bottom left, and detail right) of 1889–90 is one of the most expressive of Cézanne's works, whilst his sleeve, free from any figurative concern, is a prodigious feat of abstract art. Only the greatest have managed to combine such intense human feeling with such astonishing success in pure painting.

interesting study, so varied that I think I could be busy for months without moving from the spot and merely leaning sometimes more to the right, sometimes more to the left.' His chosen subjects remained the forest and especially Mont Sainte-Victoire, to which he gave a new look after 1900.

The portraits of Cézanne's gardener Vallier in *The Sailor* (opposite) and *Seated Man* (below) are semi-fantastic apparitions.

## An island, an eruption, an iceberg: the last *Mont Sainte-Victoires* take on a different identity

The colours are worked in an almost Impressionist manner, by the accumulation of small touches of paint, whether thinly or thickly applied. The part of the canvas that is usually called the ground, the earth, the vegetation, is totally indecipherable. With a few exceptions it is impossible to try and make out, as one could in the earlier *Sainte-Victoire* paintings, a house, a tree, an aqueduct. A clearly marked horizontal line separates the lower part of the surface, which is covered with dark greens, Prussian blues and a little brown, from the Mont Sainte-Victoire itself, which stands in isolation with its bluish, mauve or dark-green silhouette. The remainder of the upper part of the picture (where the sky can be seen) blends a more sustained blue with green.

In order to express the intense emotion he felt and mould it into harmonious form, Cézanne needed the incentive of working from nature, which always remains recognizable. He wanted, he said, to transmit his sensations, but the pictures he painted are unreal and visionary, imbued with a powerful lyricism. (He was supposed, quite wrongly, to have defective eyesight.) In his last *Sainte-Victoire* paintings, the mountain is no longer an integral part of the panorama of hills and vegetation, but a mass which is clearly separated from them. It is no longer one element of a view, part of the same world as the plain, the trees and houses; it is of a different nature. A very strongly defined horizontal line separates it from the rest of the landscape. Left: *Mont Sainte-Victoire Seen from Les Lauves* (1904–6). Opposite, from top to bottom: three views of *Mont Sainte-Victoire* (1904–6). Opposite below left: a photograph of Cézanne at his easel on the hill of Les Lauves taken in 1906 by the painter Ker-Xavier Roussel.

This reading, however, is only the result of memory projecting the image of the clearly legible *Sainte-Victoire* pictures of the preceding period on to the shape of the mountain and the sky.

In some of the *Sainte-Victoire* paintings, besides several *Château Noir* and *Bibémus* canvases, there are some green patches which could not possibly, in any figurative rendering of reality, represent branches of trees.

Here is a clear example of arbitrary placing of colour or rather of a total move away from representation of actual reality. Raoul Dufy (1877–1953), Fernand Leger (1881–1955) and many others have since made us familiar with the interest shown by modern art in form and colour, but Cézanne was the first to put his ideas into practice in a way that was shocking at the time.

### A subject is still necessary

This need to take the visible as his starting point led to Cézanne's death. On 15 October 1906 a thunderstorm took him by surprise while he was painting. He lost consciousness and was carried back home. Yet he wanted to work the next day on a portrait of his gardener, Vallier. He died from pneumonia a week later on 22 October 1906.

### The first modern painter

❛ Cézanne is one of the greatest of those who changed the course of art-history and it is inappropriate to compare him to Van Gogh or Gauguin. He brings Rembrandt to mind. Like the painter of *The Pilgrims to Emmaus,* ignoring everything marginal and incidental, he has plumbed the depths of reality with the eye of wisdom and if he himself has not arrived at those regions in which profound realism changes imperceptibly into luminous spirituality, at least he has left, for those who desire to attain it, a simple and wonderful method. He has taught us to master the vitality of the universe. He has revealed how inanimate, raw objects inflict change on one another. From him we have learned that to alter the colouring of an object is to alter its structure. His work proves without doubt that painting is not – or not any longer – the art of imitating an object by lines and colours, but of giving plastic form to our nature. ❜

Albert Gleizes and Jean Metzinger
*Du Cubisme,* 1912

# DOCUMENTS

# Friendship between artists

*It is through writers such as Joachim Gasquet and Emile Zola that we gain an impression of the artist Cézanne, his work and ideas on art, and the effect he had on others.*

### Cézanne's own voice

*Late in life Cézanne met the poet and novelist Joachim Gasquet, who later reconstructed their numerous conversations. It was hard for Cézanne to explain in words what he was trying to do in paint.*

*'All right...look at this...(He repeated his gesture, holding his hands apart, fingers spread wide, bringing them slowly, very slowly together again, then squeezing and contracting them until they were interlocked.)'*

That's what one needs to achieve...If one hand is too high, or too low, the whole thing is ruined. There mustn't be a single slack link, a single gap through which the emotion, the light, the truth can escape. I advance all of my canvas at one time, if you see what I mean. And in the same movement, with the same conviction, I approach all the scattered pieces...Everything we look at disperses and vanishes, doesn't it? Nature is always the same, and yet its appearance is always changing. It is our business as artists to convey the thrill of nature's permanence along with the elements and the appearance of all its changes. Painting must give us the flavour of nature's eternity. Everything, you understand. So I join together nature's straying hands...From all sides, here, there and everywhere, I select colours, tones and shades; I set them down, I bring them together...They make lines. They become objects – rocks, trees – without my thinking about them. They take on volume, value. If, as I perceive them, these volumes and values correspond on my canvas to the planes and patches of colour that lie before me, that appear to my eyes, well then, my canvas 'joins hands'. It holds firm. It aims neither too high nor too low. It's true, dense, full...But if there is the slightest

Cézanne around 1871.

distraction, the slightest hitch, above all if I interpret too much one day, if I'm carried away today by a theory which contradicts yesterday's, if I think while I'm painting, if I meddle, then whoosh!, everything goes to pieces.'

*Joachim Gasquet's Cézanne*
Trans. by Christopher Pemberton, 1991

## The comradeship of genius

*The roots of the friendship between the painter Cézanne and the novelist Zola lie in childhood, where dreams and desires are born. Zola certainly knew the man, but he failed to appreciate the artist and his work.*

Zola around 1860.

You are an enigma to me, a sphinx, an impossible and impenetrable mystery. One of two things is true: either you do not want to, and you are achieving your aim admirably; or you do want to, and in that case I don't understand it at all. Sometimes your letters give me hope, sometimes they rob me of that and more, like your last one, in which you almost seem to say goodbye to your dreams, which you could so easily convert into reality. In this letter, there is this sentence which I have tried in vain to understand: 'I am going to talk without saying anything, for my conduct contradicts my words.' I have constructed many hypotheses on the meaning of these words, but none satisfies me. What, then, is your behaviour? That of a lazy person no doubt; but what is surprising about that? You are being forced to do work which is distasteful to you and you want to ask your father to let you come to Paris to become an artist; I do not see any contradiction between this request and your actions. You neglect the law, you go to the museum, painting is the only work you find acceptable; there is, I think, an admirable unity between your wishes and your actions. Shall I tell you?

– but don't be angry – you lack character; you have a horror of exertion, whatever it may be, in thought as well as action; your main aim is to let things take their course and to leave yourself at the mercy of time and chance. I do not say that you are completely wrong; everyone sees things in his own way or at least believes he does. Only you have already followed this course in love; you were waiting, you said, for the right time and circumstances; you know better than I, neither one nor the other has arrived.... I thought it my duty to repeat here for the last time what I have often told you: as I am your friend, you must excuse my frankness. In many respects, our characters are similar; but, by Heaven! if I were in your place, I would want to have the last word, to risk all to gain all, and not hesitate any longer between two such different choices for my future, between art and the law. I am sorry for you, for you must be suffering in this uncertainty, and this would be for me another incentive to tear the veil from your eyes. One thing or the other, be a lawyer or an artist, but do not remain a creature without a name, wearing a toga splashed with paint.

You are a bit negligent – let me say this without making you angry – and my letters no doubt are lying about and your parents read them. I do not believe that I am giving you bad advice; I believe I speak as a friend and according to reason, but perhaps everyone does not see things as I do and if what I have suggested above is true, I am probably not very well thought of by your family. For them, I am no doubt the *liaison dangereuse,* the stone thrown on to your path to trip you up. All this affects me deeply, but, as I have told you so often, I have seen myself so often misjudged that one more wrong judgment added to the others would not surprise me. Remain my friend, that is all I desire.

Another passage of your letter grieved me. Sometimes, so you tell me, you throw your brushes at the ceiling when the results do not meet your ideas. Why this disheartened attitude, this impatience? I could understand this behaviour if it took place after years of study, after thousands of useless attempts. Recognizing your incompetence, your inability to do well, you would then act wisely if you trampled your palette, your canvas and your brushes underfoot.

But as, up to now, you have only had the wish to work, as you have not yet tackled the task seriously and regularly, you have no right to judge yourself incapable. So have courage; what you have done up to now is nothing. Have courage and remember that in order to arrive at your goal, you need years of study and perseverance. Am I not in the same position as you; is the form not just as rebellious under my fingers? We have the idea; so let us march freely and bravely on our path and may God guide us!

Emile Zola
Letter to Paul Cézanne, Paris, July 1860

I see Cézanne rarely. Alas! It is no longer as it was at Aix, when we were eighteen, free and without any worries about the future. Now the demands of our lives and our different work, keep us apart.

In the morning, Paul goes to the Atelier Suisse, while I remain in my room to write. At eleven o'clock we have lunch, each of us on our own. Sometimes, at midday, I go to his place and he works on my portrait.

Then he spends the rest of the day drawing at [Joseph] Villevieille's; he has his supper, goes to bed early and I do not see him any more.

Is that what I had hoped for? Paul is still the excellent, odd fellow whom I knew at school. To prove that he has lost none of his originality, I only have to tell you that hardly had he arrived here than he talked about returning to Aix; to have battled for three years for this trip and then not to care a straw!

Faced with such a character, with such unforeseen and such unreasonable changes of behaviour, I admit that I do not say anything and suppress any logical thought. To prove something to Cézanne would be like trying to persuade the towers of Notre-Dame to dance a quadrille. He might say yes, but he would not budge an inch. And note that age has increased his stubbornness…He is made of one single piece, obstinate and hard; nothing can bend him, nothing can wring a concession from him. He doesn't even want to discuss his thoughts; he has a horror of discussion, first, because he finds talking tiring, and then because he would have to change his view of life if his adversary were right.

Emile Zola
Letter to Baptistin Baille
Paris, 10 June 1861

*Cézanne turned to Zola for help. Several times he stayed at Médan, at Zola's house. But misunderstanding grew between the two men.*

My dear Emile,

I appeal again this month to your kindness. I would be much obliged if you could once more send sixty francs to Hortense, who is at the Vieux Chemin de Rome 12 until 12 September.

I have not yet been able to find lodgings at Marseilles because I don't want them to be too expensive. I count on spending the whole winter there if my father agrees to give me money. In this way I could continue some studies I am making at l'Estaque, which I shall not leave until the last possible moment.

Thank you in advance and with my warmest greetings to you and your family.

Paul Cézanne
Letter to Emile Zola
L'Estaque, 27 August 1878

My dear Emile,

As you tell me, I shall come to Médan on Wednesday. I shall try to start in the morning. I should have liked to be able to go on with my painting, but I was in a great state of confusion, for, as I have to go down south, I decided that the sooner I went the better. On the other hand it would perhaps be better if I waited a little. I am in a state of indecision. Perhaps I shall get out of it.

I send you my cordial greetings.

Paul Cézanne
Letter to Emile Zola
Vernon, 19 July 1885

### L'Oeuvre

*Zola never understood Cézanne's paintings, nor those of the Impressionists. In 1886 the publication of L'Oeuvre, in which Zola modelled a failed painter, Claude Lantier, on Cézanne, brought about a permanent break between the two friends.*

Such is the effort of creation that goes into the work of art! Such was the agonizing effort he had to make, the blood and tears it cost him to create living flesh to produce the breath of life! Everlastingly struggling with the Real and being repeatedly conquered like Jacob fighting with the Angel! He threw himself body and soul into the impossible task of putting all nature on one canvas and exhausted himself in the

Zola's country residence, the Château de Médan.

end by the relentless tension of his aching muscles without ever bringing forth the expected work of genius. The half-measures and trickery that satisfied other painters filled him with remorse and indignation; they were both weak and cowardly, he said. Consequently he was always starting afresh, spoiling the good in order to do better, because his painting 'didn't say anything', finding fault with his women because, as his friends used to say, they didn't step out of the canvas and sleep with him! What was it he lacked, he wondered, to make them really alive? Next to nothing, probably. Some slight adjustment one way or the other. One day, overhearing the expression 'near genius' applied to himself, he was both flattered and horrified. Yes, that must be the explanation, he thought, over-shooting or falling short of the mark through some maladjustment of the nerve centres, or through some hereditary flaw which, because of a gramme or two of substance too much or too little, instead of making him a great man was going to make him a madman. This was the notion he could never escape when despair drove him out of the studio, the notion of preordained impotence; he could feel it beating in his head with the persistence of a funeral knell...and his sympathy for Claude as a brother-artist had increased since he realized that Claude had somehow lost his foothold and, so far as his art was concerned, was slipping deeper and deeper into madness, heroic madness. At first he had been amazed, for he had had greater faith in his friend than in himself; ever since their schooldays he had considered himself inferior to Claude, whom he looked up to as one of the masters who would revolutionize the art of a whole epoch. Then his heart had been wrung by the spectacle of failing genius, and surprise had given way to bitter compassion for the unspeakable torments of impotence. Was it ever possible, in art, to say where madness lay? he wondered. Failures always moved him to tears and the more a book or a painting inclined towards aberration, the more grotesque and lamentable the artist's effort, the more he tended to radiate charity, the greater was his urge to put the stricken soul respectfully to sleep among all the wild extravagance of its dreams....

## 'To end in this'

He recalled, too, how they had all worked together in later life, their certainty of victory, their insatiable hunger for success and the feeling that they could swallow Paris in one mouthful. How often, in those days, had he seen Claude as the great man, the man whose unbridled genius would leave the talents of all the rest of them far, far behind! He remembered ... the mighty canvases they dreamed of, the projects that were going to 'shatter the Louvre', their untiring struggles, working ten hours a day, giving themselves body and soul to their art. And all to what purpose? After twenty years of passionate striving, this; this mean, sinister little object, universally ignored, isolated like a leper, a melancholy, heartbreaking sight! All the hopes, all the sufferings of a whole lifetime spent on the arduous task of bringing into the world what? This, this, this! Oh God!

Emile Zola
*L'Oeuvre: The Masterpiece*
Trans. by Thomas Walton, 1950

## The rupture

My dear Emile,
    I have just received *L'Oeuvre,* which

Cézanne and Zola at the turn of the century.

you were good enough to send me. I thank the author of *Les Rougon-Macquart* for this kind token of remembrance and ask him to allow me to shake him by the hand in memory of years gone by.

Ever yours moved by the feeling of past times.

Paul Cézanne
Letter to Emile Zola
Gardanne, 4 April 1886

# Confidences

*In this well-known family game, with its brief and occasionally brutal replies, Cézanne confides feelings or artistic ideas which are more fully developed in his letters or conversations: friendship, nature, painting and Provence. The date of these Confidences is much debated.*

Nothing here, neither furniture nor ornaments, could distract Cézanne from his sole preoccupation – painting.

NAME AND CHRISTIAN NAME:
Paul Cézanne

PLACE OF BIRTH: Aix-en-Provence

PLACE AND DATE OF THE CONFIDENCES:
On the second floor of No 30 in the rue Saint-Louis.

1.  Q: What is your favourite colour?
    *A: General harmony.*

2.  Q: What is your favourite smell?
    *A: The smell of the fields.*

3.  Q: What is your favourite flower?
    *A: Scabiosa.*

4.  Q: What animal is most appealing to you?
    *A: (No reply)*

5.  Q: What colour eyes and hair do you prefer?
    *A: (No reply)*

6.  Q: What do you consider the most estimable virtue?
    *A: Friendship.*

7.  Q: What vice do you detest most?
    *A: (No reply)*

8.  Q: What work do you prefer?
    *A: Painting.*

9.  Q: What leisure activity do you enjoy most?
    *A: Swimming.*

10. Q: What seems to you the ideal of earthly happiness?
    *A: To have 'une belle formule'.*

11. Q: What seems the worst fate to you?
    *A: To be destitute.*

12. Q: May we ask how old you are?
    *A: (No reply)*

13. Q: What Christian name would you have taken if you had the choice?
    *A: My own.*

The studio at Les Lauves, built in 1901, was only a few minutes' walk from the Mont Sainte-Victoire.

14. Q: What was the finest moment of your life?
A: *(No reply)*

15. Q: What was the most painful?
A: *(No reply)*

16. Q: What is your greatest aspiration?
A: *Certainty.*

Skulls, apples, a small statue of a plaster Cupid – all these objects followed Cézanne from one studio to another.

17. Q: Do you believe in friendship?
A: *Yes.*

18. Q: What moment of the day do you find most agreeable?
A: *The morning.*

19. Q: What historical personage are you most drawn to?
A: *Napoleon.*

20. Q: What character from literature or the theatre?
A: *Frenhoffer (sic).*

21. Q: In what region would you like to live?
A: *Provence and Paris.*

22. Q: What writer do you admire most?
A: *Racine.*

23. Q: What painter?
A: *Rubens.*

24. Q: What musician?
A: *Weber.*

25. Q: What motto would you take if you had one?
A: *(No reply)*

26. Q: What do you consider nature's masterpiece?
A: *Her infinite diversity.*

27. Q: Of what place have you retained the pleasantest memory?
A: *The hills of St Marc.*

28. Q: What is your favourite dish?
A: *Les pommes de terre à l'huile.*

29. Q: Do you like a hard bed or a soft one?
A: *In-between.*

30. Q: To the people of which foreign country are you most drawn?
A: *To none.*

*Autograph:* Write one of your own thoughts or a quotation that you agree with.

A: *Lord, you have made me strong and solitary.*
*Let me sleep the sleep of the earth.*
[*Moïse,* Alfred] de Vigny, [1797–1863]

*Cézanne by Himself*
Ed. by Richard Kendall, 1988

# The Impressionist encounter

*Through his relations with Pissarro and his friends, Cézanne learnt to master his exaggerated Romanticism and discovered the world of colour and a light palette. But, very quickly, he drew away from the Impressionists and their superficial world. As early as 1874, he wrote to his mother: 'I am beginning to think myself better than those around me.'*

### Duranty hails the 'new painting'

As far as colouring is concerned, [the Impressionists] have made a discovery of real originality, the sources of which cannot be found anywhere in the past, neither in the works of the Dutch school, nor in fresco painting, with its clear tones, nor in the light tonalities of the 18th century. They are not only concerned with that fine and subtle manipulation of colour which stems from the close and intimate observation of the most delicate tonal values which are contrary or complementary to each

Cézanne etched by Camille Pissarro in 1874.

other. Their real discovery consists in the realization that a strong light *discolours* tones, that sunshine, reflected off objects, tends by virtue of its clarity to blend its seven prismatic rays into a single, uncoloured brilliance which is light. From one flash of intuition to another, they have succeeded in breaking up solar light into its rays, its elements, and to reconstruct it as a unity by the general harmony of the iridescence they spread on their canvases. From the viewpoint of the refinement of vision and the subtle penetration of colours, it produced an extraordinary result. The most astute physicist could find no fault with their analysis of colour.... You must realize that close to the hearts of all of them in this moment is a passion for a new approach and for freedom.

Louis-Emile-Edmond Duranty
*La Nouvelle Peinture,* 1876
Quoted in *The Impressionists at First Hand,* ed. by Bernard Denvir, 1987

## Turbulent passions mastered by the structure of colours

It was because he never integrated or because he rejected the style of the artists he admired that Cézanne could show the strength of his originality from the beginning of his career. The slow process of absorbing the lessons of the masters inhibits young artists' means of expression in the first place. Only the present sanctification of art allows these clumsy attempts, where there is both pathos and rhetoric, to be taken as aesthetic successes.

In this respect, Cézanne's encounter with the Impressionists was to be crucial. He became a close friend of Pissarro. Being ten years older, this humble and generous man did not frighten Cézanne. But, even though he had known Pissarro for several years, it was only in 1872

that he set up his easel by Pissarro's side. Pissarro and the Impressionists after him turned to open-air painting, observation of nature and had discovered a space no longer founded on geometry but structured by the play of light on the forms it fragmented. This influence allowed Cézanne to give up his research into the expression of the passions which was leading him nowhere. It channelled him towards observation of a subject in some ways nullified by the effort of understanding. By teaching him to be bound by his own sensations in the face of nature, Pissarro opened up a line of research he was to follow all his life. He became a model of freedom, forgetting what had happened before him and discovering his own personal method

$P$*issarro on his Way to Work* (c. 1874).

of representation. Pissarro liberated him from the obsession with form, an area where he was a failure, while his drawing was impelled by the strength of his passions…. Cézanne, who up until then had been a dilettante, said in 1871: 'When I really understood Pissarro, I developed a passion for work.' He summed up this lesson in this way: 'I wanted to copy nature but did not succeed; but I was very pleased with myself when I discovered that it had to be represented through something else… through colour.' Forms were no longer born of contours, colour was to be the basis of representation, the object was to be reborn through the contrast of colours: 'There is no such thing as line… there are only contrasts…of colour.'

An immediate effect to be noted was the blossoming of his senses due to the unfurling of his gifts as a superb colourist. The elimination of turbulent passions allowed his sensuality to blossom and luminosity and happiness replaced heavy, sombre tones. Violence, which led to furious and encrusted brushstrokes, made way for a patient working method that structured the canvas by the juxtaposition of small coloured strokes.

Michel Artières
*Menace d'objet et saisie du motif*
5 September 1984

### Searching for the structure of things

Consequently, Cézanne studied effects of light and air and tried to convey them through color; he learned that objects have no specific color of their own, but reflect each other, and that air intervenes between eye and object. Cézanne not only made these observations on nature but also expressed them in his still-lifes. The first of these, painted in Auvers, still reveal some of Manet's influence and are in somber tones: dull yellows and reds against absolutely black backgrounds. Cézanne painted them in Dr Gachet's studio and chose as subjects glasses, bottles, knives and other not very colorful objects…. But Cézanne soon tired of the limited range of whitish browns and the grays that predominate in these compositions and began to paint the flowers that Madame Gachet picked for him in her garden. These little canvases have remarkably clear and vibrant colors: blues, reds, and yellows of extraordinary intensity that bear witness to the pleasure he felt in rendering such richness of tone….

As Cézanne developed his art, he detached himself increasingly from the Impressionist conceptions. He did not seek to capture the impression and vibrant atmosphere of a landscape but rather to portray its forms and colors, its planes and light. He did not approve of Monet's attempts to render the same subject at different times of the day, to show the different shapes and tints produced by the varying intensity of the sun. Nor did he approve of the efforts of 'the humble and colossal' Pissarro, as he called him admiringly, who was then being attracted by the Divisionism of Georges Seurat and painting his pictures in the pointillist technique…. As for Renoir, Cézanne did not like his landscape technique, which he called 'cottony'. Altogether he had the impression that his friends experimented too much, that they did not look behind the colorful exterior for the actual structure of things; it is doubtless for this reason that he assumed the task of 'making out of Impressionism something solid and durable like the art of museums'.

John Rewald
*Cézanne: A Biography*, 1986

In the garden of the master Impressionist Camille Pissarro (standing right) at Pontoise in 1877 are, among others, Cézanne (seated left) and Lucien Pissarro (boy).

# Cézanne expresses his opinions on painting

*Cézanne faced the problem of whether to exhibit or to work in silence. He chose to withdraw from public life very soon, to live like a hermit while painting and to have only one master and one model: nature. This choice is expressed in his letters.*

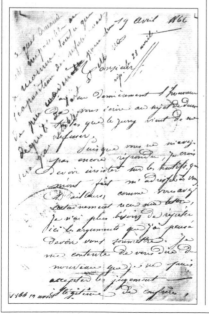

*Cézanne wanted his work to be judged by the public and not by the juries and critics of the official Salons whom he despised.*

### To Count de Nieuwerkerke, Director of Fine Arts

Dear Sir,

I recently had the honour of writing to you about two paintings of mine which the jury of the Salon turned down.

As you have not answered me, I feel I must remain firm about the motives which led me to address you. Moreover, as you have certainly received my letter, there is no need for me to repeat the arguments that I thought necessary to submit to you. I content myself with saying again that I cannot accept the unjustified criticism of fellow-artists whom I have not myself expressly asked to appraise me.

I am therefore writing to you to insist on my request. I want to appeal to the public and have an exhibition all the same. My wish does not seem to me to be at all outrageous and, if you were to ask all those painters in my position, they would all reply that they rejected the jury and that they wished to take part in one way or another in an exhibition which should perforce be open to every genuine working artist.

Therefore let the Salon des Refusés be re-established. Even were I to be there alone, I should still ardently wish that people should at least know that I no more want to be mixed up with those gentlemen of the jury than they seem to want to be mixed up with me.

I trust, Monsieur, that you will not continue to keep silent. It seems to me that every decent letter deserves a reply.

I beg to remain, Sir, yours very faithfully.

Paul Cézanne
2 Rue Beautreillis, Paris, 19 April 1866

## To Octave Maus (1856–1919), the Belgian art-critic and organiser of the Cercle des Vingt and Les Vingt in Brussels

Dear Sir,

Having learnt the contents of your flattering letter, I should like to thank you first and then accept your kind invitation with pleasure.

May I, however, be permitted to refute the accusation of disdain which you attribute to me with reference to my refusal to take part in exhibitions of painting?

I must tell you with regard to this matter that, as the many studies to which I have dedicated myself have given only negative results, and as I am afraid of only too justified criticism, I had resolved to work in silence until the day when I should feel myself able to defend theoretically the result of my attempts.

However, in view of the pleasure in finding myself in such good company, I do not hesitate to alter my resolve and I beg you, Monsieur, to accept my thanks and good wishes.

Paul Cézanne
Paris, 27 November 1889

## To Joachim Gasquet (1873–1921), poet and novelist

But I curse the Geffroys and the few characters who, for the sake of writing an article for 50 francs, have drawn the attention of the public to me. All my life I have worked to be able to earn my living, but I thought that I could do good painting without attracting attention to my private life. Certainly, an artist wishes to raise himself intellectually as much as possible, but the man himself must remain obscure. The pleasure must be found in the work. If it had been given to me to realize my aim, I should have remained in my corner with the few studio companions with whom we used to go out for a drink. I still have a good friend [probably Achille Emperaire] from that time. Well, he has not been successful, a fact which does not prevent him from being a bloody sight better painter than all the daubers, with the medals and decorations which make one sick; and you want me at my age to believe in anything?

Paul Cézanne
Aix, 30 April 1896

*Cézanne was finishing the portrait of Joachim Gasquet's father, Henri. Gasquet recorded Cézanne's thoughts during the sittings.*

Ah, everyone knows his own troubles…As far as I'm concerned I know you because I'm painting you… I tell you, Henri, what you have is certainty. That's my great ambition. To be sure! Every time I attack a canvas I feel convinced, I believe that something's going to come of it…But I immediately remember that I've always failed before. Then I taste blood…Now take you, for instance, you know what's good and what's bad in life, and you follow your own path…But me – I never know where I'm going or where I want to go with this damned profession. All the theories mess you up inside…Is it because I'm timid in life? Basically, if you have character you have talent…I don't mean to say that character is enough, that it's enough to be a good fellow in order to paint well…That would make it too easy…But I don't believe that a scoundrel can have genius.

*Joachim Gasquet's Cézanne: A Memoir with Conversations*
Trans. by Christopher Pemberton, 1991
Originally published 1921

## To a young artist

I have perhaps come too early. I was the painter of your generation more than of my own.... You are young, you have vitality; you will impart to your art an impetus which only those who have emotion can give. As for myself, I feel I am getting old. I shall not have time to express myself...Let's work!...Perception of the model and its realization are sometimes very long in coming.

Paul Cézanne, c. 1896

## To Charles Camion (b. 1879), Fauve painter

[Thomas] Couture used to say to his pupils: 'Keep good company, that is: go to the Louvre. But after having seen the great masters who repose there, we must hurry out and, by contact with nature, revive within ourselves the instincts, the artistic sensations which live within us.'

Paul Cézanne
Aix, 13 September 1903

## To Emile Bernard (1868–1941), leader of the school of Pont-Aven

May I repeat what I told you here: treat nature by means of the cylinder, the sphere, the cone, with everything in proper perspective so that each side of an object or plane is directed towards a central point. Lines parallel to the horizon give breadth, that is a section of nature, or, if you prefer, of the spectacle which the *pater omnipotens aeterne deus* spreads before our eyes. Lines perpendicular to this horizon give depth. But nature for us is more depth than surface, from where comes the need to introduce into our light vibrations, represented by the reds and yellows, enough blue to give the feel of air.

Paul Cézanne
Aix, 15 April 1904

I proceed very slowly, for nature reveals herself to me in very complex ways and there is endless progress to be made. One must look at the model and feel very

T he Musée Granet at Aix-en-Provence.

exactly; and also express oneself distinctly and with force. Taste is the best judge. It is rare. Art addresses itself only to a very limited number of individuals.

The artist must scorn all judgment that is not based on intelligent observation of character. He must beware of the literary spirit which so often causes the painter to deviate from his true path – the concrete study of nature – to lose himself too long in intangible speculation.

The Louvre is a good book to consult but it must be only an intermediary. The real and great study to be undertaken is the manifold picture of nature....

Paul Cézanne
Aix, 12 May 1904

## To his son

Finally, I must tell you that as a painter I am becoming more clear-sighted before nature, but that I always find the realization of my sensations painful. I cannot attain the intensity that is unfolded before my senses. I do not have the magnificent richness of colouring that animates nature. Here on the banks of the river there are so many subjects and the same one seen from a different angle makes a powerful and interesting study, so varied that I think I could be busy for months without moving from the spot and merely leaning sometimes more to the right, sometimes more to the left. I believe the young painters to be much more intelligent than the rest, the old painters can only see a disastrous rival in me.

Paul Cézanne
Aix, 8 September 1906

[Charles] Camoin showed me a photograph of a figure by the unfortunate Emile Bernard; we are all agreed on this point, that he is an intellectual saturated with memories from museums, but who does not look enough at nature, and that is the great thing, to make himself free from the school and indeed all schools. So that Pissarro was not mistaken, though he went a little far, when he said that all the necropolises of art should be burnt down.

Certainly one could make a strange menagerie with all the professionals of art and their kindred spirits....

Paul Cézanne
Aix, 26 September 1906

In *Polyphemus* (1649) by Nicolas Poussin – which Cézanne declared he wished 'to imbue... with life by contact with nature' – the mountain dominates but does not totally crush people.

# Views of the critics

*'Crude experiments…
Disgusting filth…
Impulsive, meaningless art,
crazy as a savage… A
hopeless failure…'
While painters recognized
and admired Cézanne, the
critics, with few exceptions,
hardly spared him, even
after his death.*

T*he Strangled Woman* (c. 1870–2) displays the theatrical composition of *A Modern Olympia* (c. 1873) that so appalled the critics at the first Impressionist exhibition of 1874.

### The first Impressionist exhibition, Paris, 1874

Shall we talk of M. Cézanne? Of all known juries, not one has ever imagined, even in dreams, the possibility of accepting any work by this painter who came to the Salon carrying his canvases on his back like Jesus carried his cross. A too consuming love of yellow has up to now compromised M. Cézanne's future.

Ernest d'Hervilly
*Le Rappel,* 17 April 1874

Suddenly he gave a great cry when he saw *The House of the Hanged Man* by M. Paul Cézanne. The stupendous thick fleshy impasto of this little jewel completed the work begun with the *Boulevard des Capucines;* old father Vincent would be delirious.…

'Don't talk to me about *A Modern Olympia,* there's a good fellow!

'Alas! just go and see that one. There is a woman bent in two with a black woman lifting the last veil to present her in all her ugliness to a brown puppet. Do you remember Manet's *Olympia?* Well, that was a masterpiece of drawing, of propriety, of finished work compared to M. Cézanne's picture.'

At last the vessel overflowed. The classical mind of old father Vincent, attacked from too many sides at once, became completely unhinged. He stopped in front of the Parisian keeper of all these treasures and, taking him for a portrait, began to criticize him in a very pronounced way.

'Is he ugly enough?' he said shrugging his shoulders. 'From the front he has two eyes…and a nose…and a mouth!… The Impressionists wouldn't have bothered with all that detail. With all that time and energy wasted on useless things, Monet could have painted twenty Parisian keepers!'

'Keep moving there, you,' the 'portrait' said to him.

'Just listen to that! He can even speak! That must have taken the beggar who daubed him some time to do!'

Louis Leroy
'The Exhibition of the Impressionists'
*Le Charivari*, 25 April 1874

### The third Impressionist exhibition, Paris, 1877

The artist who has been the most attacked, the most badly treated by the press and public for the past fifteen years, is M. Cézanne. There is no scurrilous epithet which has not been coupled with his name, and his works have the success of a howling farce, and continue to do so,... In his works, M. Cézanne is a Greek of the golden age; his canvases have the calm and heroic serenity of the paintings and terracottas of antiquity, and the ignorant people who laugh at *The Bathers*, for example, make me think of barbarians criticizing the Parthenon.

M. Cézanne is a painter and a great painter. Those who have never wielded a paintbrush or a pencil have said he did not know how to draw and they have reproached him for imperfections which are in fact subtle refinements achieved through enormous skill.

I know that, in spite of all, M. Cézanne cannot achieve the success of painters in fashion.... However, M. Cézanne's painting has the unutterable charm of biblical and Greek antiquity, the movements of people are simple and great as in antique sculpture, the landscapes possess compelling majesty, and his still-lifes, which are so beautiful and so exact in their harmony of tones, have a solemn quality of truth. In all his paintings, the artist moves us, because he himself experiences, by observing nature,

a violent emotion which his craftsmanship transmits to the canvas.

Georges Rivière
*L'Impressioniste*, 14 April 1877

### The Salon d'Automne, Paris, 1904

What at first sight singles out M. Cézanne's painting is clumsy drawing and heavy colours. His still-lifes, which have been much praised, are coarsely rendered and lifeless. It has been predicted that they will one day go to the Louvre and keep company with Chardin. This happy time is not imminent.

M. Fouquier
*Le Journal*, 14 October 1904

Ah! Cézanne! Blessed are the poor in spirit, for the heaven of art is theirs! But truly, corrupt as we are, why compose, draw and paint? Why seek to know when it is so voluptuous to feel? Why speak of education, instruction, erudition, since art is immediate, impulsive, meaningless and mad as a hatter?

M. Bouyer
*La Revue Bleue*, 5 November 1904

I see that the Cézannes have had a great success at the Salon d'Automne – it was about time!

Mary Cassatt
Letter to Théodore Duret
30 November 1904

### The Salon d'Automne, Paris, 1905

What do they still want with M. Paul Cézanne? Is his cause really not listened to? Doesn't everyone who has seen his works consider him a complete failure? Too bad for the dealers who thought, because of Zola's belief, that there would be a good deal to be made from his works. M. Vollard should come to a decision!...

Camille Mauclair
*La Lanterne*, 19 October 1905

As for M. Cézanne, his name will remain linked to the most memorable joke in art for these last fifteen years. It has taken all the 'Cockney impudence' of which Ruskin speaks, to invent the 'genius' of this honest old man who paints for pleasure in the provinces and produces heavy works, which are badly constructed though some conscientiously at times. He also produces still-lifes of moderately beautiful subjects and rather crude colouring, landscapes of lead, and figures which a journalist recently called 'like Michaelangelo's' but which are quite simply the shapeless experiments of a man who has not been able to substitute good will for know-how.

Camille Mauclair
*La Revue,* 15 December 1905

## The Salon d'Automne, Paris, 1906: Cézanne retrospective

To deny that Cézanne is one of the most conscious, one of the most serious and one of the most individual masters of today, is to deny the evidence. To treat him as a 'clever mason', as a quaint, wild drawer of pictures, who 'sees crooked' in front of nature, is not tenable any longer. The joke has really lasted too long. Just the same, who the devil would dream of denying his faults: uneven, stumbling, clumsy, shapes which are warped, back-grounds which move forward, planes which are turned upside down, lopsided characters. We know all that. But does Rubens have taste, and Renoir ideas?

Louis Vauxcelles
*Gil Blas,* 5 October 1906

## Grafton Galleries, London, 1905

'Hullo! What's this? What are these funny brown-and-olive landscapes doing in an Impressionist exhibition? Brown! I ask you? Isn't it absurd for a man to go on using brown and call himself an Impressionist painter? Who are they by? Oh, Cézanne. That's the man who paints still-life. Now, I like those better. Those apples over there are really very good. And this other thing, *Dessert.* That's not so bad. The apple's quite good, isn't it? and the knife. But that right-hand side of the flask is pretty wobbly, and that glass hasn't quite come off. He's not very strong on drawing, is he? But I like his draperies, that curtain and the table-cloth; and the table too, that's really quite good. Yes, there's something in it, but it's rather dark and brown. I don't like his colour. Let's go back and look at the Monets.'

That is how the 'fans' of Impressionist painting talked about Cézanne in 1905.

Frank Rutter
*Art in my Time,* 1933

## Grafton Galleries, London, 1910

To the Grafton Gallery to look at what are called the Post-Impressionist pictures sent over from Paris. The exhibition is either an extremely bad joke or a swindle. I am inclined to think the latter, for there is no trace of humour in it. Still less is there a trace of sense or skill or taste, good or bad, or art or cleverness. Nothing but that gross puerility which scrawls indecencies on the walls of a privy. The drawing is on the level of that of an untaught child of seven or eight years old, the sense of colour that of a teatray painter, the method that of a schoolboy who wipes his fingers on a slate after spitting on them. There is nothing at all more humorous than that, at all more clever. In all the 300 or 400 pictures there was not one worthy of attention even by its singularity, or appealing to any feeling but of disgust.

Wilfrid Scawen Blunt
Diary entry for 15 November 1910
*My Diaries,* 1920

* He was a large and handsome fellow with long, dark-brown hair and a beard of the same colour, which was naturally curly. His slightly aquiline nose and his big black eyes resulted in giving him a certain resemblance to the characters in the Assyrian bas-reliefs in the Louvre. He did not look like this for long. A few years later, he was bald on top, his beard and hair were cut shorter and were already sprinkled with grey hairs, but his eyes had kept their brilliance. In his last years, his appearance had changed again. Those who knew him in the last phase of his life are in agreement in describing him as an old retired officer. ⁹

Georges Rivière, *Le Maître Paul Cézanne*, 1923

# Homage and heritage

*In the history of painting, Cézanne is one of the only artists who gathers as many judgments and tributes from the greatest painters of his time as from the greatest of his successors. Cézanne, the solitary artist, is one of those who have changed the course of history.*

Three Bathers (1879–82), a painting bought by Matisse in 1889.

## THE TRIBUTE OF HIS CONTEMPORARIES...

Cézanne's effect upon his contemporaries is already apparent in certain early works by Pissarro, his chosen mentor. But the first major figure of his generation to benefit significantly from it was Gauguin, one of the earliest collectors of Cézanne's pictures, among them the *Still-life with Compotier*, which Gauguin valued above all other works in his collection. This admiration led him, in 1890, to paint a portrait of an unknown woman [see p. 52b] seated in a pose familiar from Cézanne's portraits of his wife of the 1880s, against a background featuring the *Compotier* still-life. In further homage to the elder master, Gauguin adopts Cézanne's parallel, 'constructive' brushwork in this picture, though he simplifies the colour modulations in the *Still-life* in keeping with the more two-dimensional concerns of his own style. He thus drew attention to the decorative features of Cézanne's art, which were soon to make him one of the spiritual leaders of the Symbolist painters of the 1890s who had initially found inspiration in Gauguin.

Included among these were Emile Bernard and Maurice Denis, the latter of whom acknowledged Cézanne's importance for the group in his *Homage to Cézanne*. Exhibited in Paris in 1901, this shows a gathering of Cézanne's admirers and disciples – including Redon, Bonnard, Vuillard, and Sérusier, in addition to Denis – around the *Still-life with Compotier*. The result is a homage to Cézanne comparable to the latter's *Apotheosis of Delacroix*. Deeply touched by this tribute from the younger generation, Cézanne wrote to Denis expressing his gratitude in June 1901. 'Perhaps this will give you some idea of the position as a painter which you

Gathered round a still-life which had once belonged to Gauguin, Maurice Denis, his wife, Odilon Redon, the Nabis painters Pierre Bonnard, Edouard Vuillard, Paul Sérusier, Paul-Elié Ranson and Ker-Xavier Roussel, the critic André Mellerio and the art dealer Ambroise Vollard all pay homage to Cézanne in Denis' painting of 1900.

occupy in our time,' replied Denis, 'of the admiration which you evoke and of the enlightened enthusiasm of a group of young people to which I belong and who can rightly call themselves your pupils, as they owe to you everything which they know about painting.'

When Denis wrote, Cézanne's canvases still remained relatively inaccessible to a wide public. With the major showings of his works which took place in Paris in 1904–6, however, his crucial importance for artists of the younger generation became increasingly apparent. This was confirmed by the two memorial exhibitions devoted to the artist in 1907, the years after his death, when 79 watercolours were exhibited at

Bernheim Jeune in June and 56 oils and watercolours at the Salon d'Automne in October. (It was the latter of these exhibitions that made such a profound impression upon Rilke.)

Even before these commemorative events, Cézanne had attracted the attention of three of the pioneers of early 20th-century art, Matisse, Picasso, and Braque. Unlike their Symbolist predecessors, who were principally drawn to the decorative elements in Cézanne's style, these masters were instead attracted to its most architectonic features.

For Matisse, who purchased Cézanne's [*Three*] *Bathers* in 1899, Cézanne became a model of order and clarity in painting, whose example spurred him to explore effects of solidity and relief in his own art in the years around 1900.... Though other artists of his time drew more far-reaching conclusions from Cézanne's art, Matisse alone maintained a lifelong interest in it which was truly comprehensive and deserves to be seen as Cézanne's rightful heir. For not only did he choose to follow his great predecessor in working directly from nature but he remained aware of the equal importance which Cézanne had accorded to both form and colour in building up the armature of a picture.

But it was left for the creators of Cubism, Picasso and Braque, to investigate the most radical implications of Cézanne's style – its analytical approach to form and its rhythmic accentuation of the entire picture surface through a series of interpenetrating shapes and colours which generate space while also stressing the autonomy of the picture plane....

Cézanne himself had anticipated this development when he referred to his own painting as 'the logical development of everything we see' – implying by this a mental alteration of a visual sensation done in the interests of the compositional structure of a picture. In his art, however, this still took place before a motif in nature and was intended to reveal an invisible truth about it. But in the art of his Cubist followers it came increasingly to be done without any reference to the visible world, thus severing that link with perceived reality that had united artists from Giotto to Cézanne and paving the way for the conceptual art of our own age.

Richard Verdi
*Cézanne*, 1992

## Paul Gauguin (1848–1903)

*Although ostensibly describing Cézanne, Gauguin was in fact describing himself; you only have to replace Virgil by Maori legends.*

Look at Cézanne the Misunderstood: an essentially mystical, oriental temperament (his face looks like an old man from the Levant). He is partial to forms that exude the mystery and the tranquillity of a man lying down to dream. His sombre colours are in keeping with the oriental frame of mind. A man of the Midi, he spends entire days on mountaintops reading Virgil and gazing at the sky. Thus his horizons are very high, his blues very intense, his reds stunningly vibrant.

Like Virgil, who has more than one meaning and can be interpreted as you like, the literature of his paintings has a parabolic, twofold meaning. His backgrounds are as imaginative as they are real.

Letter to Emile Schuffenecker
Copenhagen, 14 January 1885

Cézanne in 1906.

## Claude Monet (1840–1926)

It's agreed for Wednesday. *

I hope Cézanne will still be here and that he will join the party, but he is so odd, so fearful of seeing new faces that I am afraid he may be absent in spite of his earnest wish to get to know you. What a shame this man has not had more support in his life! He is a real artist but one who has doubted himself far too much. He needs cheering up, that's why he appreciated your article so much!

Letter to Gustave Geffroy
Giverny, 23 November 1894

* Monet invited Geffroy to Giverny to meet Cézanne at a lunch on 28 November 1894.

## Camille Pissarro (1830–1903)

I was also thinking of Cézanne's show, in which there are some exquisite things, some still-lifes of irreproachable perfection, others much worked on and yet left unfinished, and, even more beautiful than the rest, some landscapes, some nudes, some unfinished heads which are, however, truly imposing and so artistic, so supple…Why?? Because sensation is there.

Letter to his son Lucien
Paris, 21 November 1895

Can you believe it, Heymann has had the cheek to put around the absurd story that Cézanne was influenced all the time by [Armand] Guillaumin? We just have to hope the public won't be taken in by it? It's the limit, and it all happened at Vollard's. Vollard was flabbergasted. Bah! Let sheep piss, as they say in Montfoucault. Isn't all this gossip amusing?

You have no idea how hard it is to make some patrons and friends of the Impressionists understand how many great and rare qualities there are in Cézanne. I believe centuries will pass before they realize it. Degas and Renoir are in raptures about Cézanne's works. Vollard showed me a drawing of some fruit. They spun a coin to know who would be the happy owner. Degas passionate about Cézanne's drawings, what do you think about that? Didn't I take a correct view of things in 1861, when [Francesco] Oller and I went to see this peculiar Provençal in the Atelier Suisse where Cézanne was painting some studies from the nude. He was the butt of all those impotent men of the school, among them that notorious [Maurice] Jacquet, wallowing in the pretty-pretty for many a year, whose works were being paid for in gold!!

It's very amusing, this re-awakening of old battles!

Letter to his son Lucien
Paris, 4 December 1895

### … AND THAT OF HIS HEIRS

## Paul Signac (1863–1935), painter and theorist in Neo-Impressionism

The brushstroke of Cézanne is the line which unites the Impressionists' method of execution with the Neo-Impressionists'. The principle – held in common but applied differently – of a mixture of points of view links these three generations of colourists who all pursue, by similar techniques, light, colour and harmony.

D'Eugene Delacroix au Néo-Impressionisme, 1899

## Paul Sérusier (1865–1927), founder of the Nabis group

Cézanne knew how to strip pictorial art of all the mould which had accumulated there through time. He showed that imitation is only a means, that the only goal is to place lines and colours on a given surface, so as to please the eye, to talk to the spirit, to create in fact, by purely plastic means, a language or rather to find once more the universal language. He is accused of uncouthness, of coldness; these are the outer trappings of his power, his apparent shortcomings! His thought is so clear in his mind! His desire to give utterance so compelling! If a tradition is born of our time – which I dare to hope it will be – it is from Cézanne that it will spring. Others, clever cooks, will then come along to make his left-overs into more modern sauces; but it is he who will have given the marrow. It is not a question of a new kind of art, but of the resurrection of all arts which are *solid and pure and classical.*

'What do you think of Cézanne?'
*Mercure de France,* 1905

## Paul Klee (1879–1940), painter, for a time part of the Blaue Reiter group

I have been able to see eight of Cézanne's paintings at the Secession [of Vienna]. Here is, for me, the master *par excellence,* the very person to instruct me, much more so than Van Gogh.

*Diary,* 1908

## Georges Rouault (1871–1958), French Expressionist painter

Do not come near me, do not touch me: I carry within me all the beauty that the world does not know, or fails to recognize. Do not come near me, do not speak to me: words and deeds are empty, I am silent, old and powerless, all my efforts are aimed at Truth and Beauty. Essentially because of this, I have been forced to live far from men, I have had to meditate and to suffer in order to accomplish what I had to do here.

'Making Cézanne speak'
*Mercure de France,* 1910

## Roger Fry (1866–1934), English painter and critic

I always admired Cézanne, but since I have had the opportunity to examine his pictures here [at the Grafton Galleries] at leisure, I feel that he is incomparably greater than I had supposed. His work has the baffling mysterious quality of the greatest originators in art. It has that supreme spontaneity as though he had almost made himself the passive, half-conscious instrument of some directing power. So little seems implied at first sight in his apparently accidental collocation of form and colour, so much reveals itself gradually to the fascinated gaze. And he was the great genius of the whole movement; he it was who discovered by some mysterious process the way out of the cul-de-sac into which the pursuit of naturalism *à outrance* had led art. As I understand his art, and I admit it is exceedingly subtle and difficult to analyse – what happened was that Cézanne, inheriting from the Impressionists the general notion of accepting the purely visual patchwork of appearance, concentrated his imagination so intensely upon certain oppositions of tone and colour that he became able to build up and, as it were, re-create form from within; and at the same time that he re-created form he re-created it clothed with colour, light and atmosphere all at once. It is this astonishing synthetic power that amazes me in his work. His composition at first sight looks accidental, as though he had sat down before any odd corner of nature and portrayed it; and yet the longer one looks the more satisfactory are the correspondences one discovers, the more certainly felt beneath its subtlety, is the architectural plan; the more absolute, in spite of their astounding novelty, do we find the colour harmonies. In a picture like *L'Estaque* it is difficult to know whether one admires more the imaginative grasp which has rebuilt so clearly for the answering mind the splendid structure of the bay, or the intellectualized sensual power which has given to the shimmering atmosphere so definite a value. He sees the face of Nature as though it were cut in some incredibly precious crystalline substance, each of its facets different, yet each dependent on the rest. When Cézanne turns to the human form he becomes, being of a supremely classic temperament, not indeed a deeply psychological painter, but one who seizes individual character in its broad, static outlines. His portrait of his wife has, to my mind, the great monumental quality of early art, of Piero della Francesca or Mantegna. It has that self-contained inner life, that resistance and assurance that belong to a real image, not to a mere reflection of some more insistent reality. Of his still-life it is hardly necessary to speak, so widespread is the recognition of his supremacy in this. Since Chardin no one has treated the casual things of daily life with such reverent and penetrating imagination, or has found as he has, in the statement of their material qualities, a language that passes altogether beyond their actual associations with common use and wont.

'The Post-Impressionists – 2', *Nation*
3 December 1910

### Walter Sickert (1860–1942), founder of the Camden Town Group

*This article is taken from the lecture in the Grafton Galleries in London just before the close of the exhibition.*

Cézanne was fated, as his passion was immense, to be immensely neglected, immensely misunderstood, and now, I think, immensely overrated. Two causes, I suspect, have been at work in the reputation his work now enjoys. I mean two causes, after all acknowledgment made of a certain greatness in his talent. The moral weight of his single-hearted and unceasing effort, of his sublime love for his art, has made itself felt. In some mysterious way, indeed, this gigantic sincerity impresses, and holds even those who have not the slightest knowledge of what were his qualities, of what he was driving at, of what he achieved, or of where he failed.

'Post-Impressionists', *Fortnightly Review*
January 1911

### Albert Gleizes (1881–1953) and Jean Metzinger (1883–1956), French Cubist painters and publicists

Cézanne is one of the greatest of those who changed the course of art-history

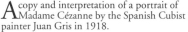

A copy and interpretation of a portrait of Madame Cézanne by the Spanish Cubist painter Juan Gris in 1918.

and it is inappropriate to compare him to Van Gogh or Gauguin. He brings Rembrandt to mind. Like the painter of *The Pilgrims of Emmaus*, ignoring everything marginal and incidental, he has plumbed the depths of reality with the eye of wisdom and if he himself has not arrived at those regions in which profound realism changes imperceptibly into luminous spirituality, at least he has left, for those who desire to attain it, a simple and wonderful method.

He has taught us to master the vitality of the universe. He has revealed how inanimate, raw objects inflict change on one another. From him we have learned that to alter the colouring of an object is to alter its structure. His work proves without doubt that painting is not – or not any longer – the art of imitating an object by lines and colours, but of giving plastic form to our nature.

To understand Cézanne is to foresee Cubism.

*Du Cubisme*, 1912

### Robert Ross (1869–1918), art critic and literary executor of Oscar Wilde

*This article was written on the Post-Impressionist exhibition in the Grafton Galleries in which approximately 30 watercolours by Cézanne were included.*

Like the Impressionists, Cézanne was constantly occupied with reality and tried to see it without any artistic prejudice; but he also incessantly tried to discover in it designs of abstract grandeur to which he would sacrifice all irrelevant fact, as the Impressionists sacrificed irrelevant fact to the facts which interested them. Both he and they maintained the freedom of the artist; but he made a different use of it. He was not so much interested in any fact for its own sake as in a kind of music for the eye which he sought for in all facts and to which he subordinated them all. In this respect he was like many artists whom we call decorative; but he differed also from most of these in one important particular. The tendency of most decorative painting is to reduce everything to two dimensions. This is carried to its furthest point in pure pattern, as in a Persian carpet, where there is no representation at all, but only an abstract music for the eye.

But Cézanne's designs, however abstract, were always conceived in three dimensions; his music was a music of masses, not of lines or flat spaces. That is what makes his art original and at the same time difficult. For we are used to think of all the means by which mass is represented as means of pure illusion. We can see a harmony of pattern easily enough, because we are used to the sacrifices of fact necessary to produce it. But we are not used either to harmonies of mass or to the sacrifices of fact necessary to produce them; and so pictures like Cézanne's *Rocks* may seem to us both meaningless and unbeautiful. They do not remind us either of rocks themselves or of a Persian carpet; they have neither illusion nor music for the eye. But Cézanne had learnt to compose in abstract masses as Cimabue [c. 1240–1302] could compose in lines and flat spaces, and he drew these masses without any design of producing an illusion of three dimensions, but only so as to reveal the new kind of music which he found in them. If, then, we are to understand his works and to see their beauty, we must not look for flat pattern in them nor must we look for the kind of abstract design that goes with flat pattern. We must accustom ourselves to abstractions in three dimensions, to a new music of masses, which at first is very disconcerting to the eye.

'Cézanne and the Post-Impressionists'
*The Times*, 8 January 1913
(unsigned but probably by Robert Ross)

## André Lhote (1885–1962), French Cubist

Let us admit that there is nothing, in all that has been attempted during these last twenty years, which does not find its point of departure in Cézanne, and what is more, sometimes, its solution in advance. Those among us who had the most far-reaching creative spirit could only emphasize the most secret intentions of the master, and give more freedom to his actions, which were often restrained by excessive modesty.

*La Peinture, le cœur et l'esprit*, 1920

## Maurice Denis (1870–1943), leader of the Nabis group

There is something paradoxical in Cézanne's fame; and it is no easier to explain than Cézanne himself. The Cézanne case irremediably divides into two camps – those who love painting and those who prefer its allied pleasures, literary or otherwise, to painting itself....

The mystery with which the master of

**B**athers (1890–4), a painting which once belonged to Maurice Denis.

Aix-en-Provence surrounded himself all his life has significantly contributed to the increasing obscurity of the commentaries that have themselves contributed to his fame. He is shy, independent, a recluse. Totally occupied with his art, perpetually anxious and usually dissatisfied with himself, he escaped public curiosity up to his last years. Those indeed who drew on the inspiration of his methods usually did not know him.

At a time when the sensibility of the artist was held almost unanimously to be the sole reason for the work of art, and when improvisation – this 'spiritual giddiness originating in the exaltation of the senses' – tended to destroy the out-of-date academic conventions and the necessary methods, it so happened that Cézanne's art was able to keep the essential role of sensibility, while at the same time substituting reflection for empiricism. For example, instead of mechanically noting phenomena, he was able to keep the feeling of the moment, though he overworked almost excessively, by planned and deliberate effort, at his studies from nature. He *composed* his still-lifes, purposely altering lines and mass, placing draperies according to premeditated rhythms, avoiding the accidents of chance, seeking plastic beauty, but without losing the true *motif*. This initial motif was to be captured in his sketches and his watercolours; I mean by this the delicate symphony of lights and shades, placed side by side, which his eye discovered at once but which his reason then spontaneously supported with a logical composition or an architectural plan.

*Théories*, 1920

## Kazimir Malevich (1878–1935), Russian painter

Cézanne, one of the strongest of those who sense the element of painting in the artist, has the same reproaches thrown at him as the Impressionists. They say that Cézanne does not master the form of his drawings and cannot cope with sketches of the model. And in both Cézannism and Impressionism we meet the same question of lack of correspondence between the form and colour of a work, the form and colour of the model.

The paintings of Cézanne and the other artists of new art give us only signs of objects, which are greatly deformed in the interests of 'art as such'. The philistines among the critics regard this deformation as a fault, arising from an inability to draw and paint. In this way all the critics lose sight of the main point – the sensation arising from this or that attitude to the object and the changes in it.

In reality, things are completely the other way round: Cézanne is a great master because he was able to express painterly sensations in their pure form.... Cézannism is one of the greatest achievements in the history of painting on account of its pure definition of painterly *Weltanschauung*.

In the personality of Cézanne our history of painting reaches the apogee of its development.

There is one self-portrait by Cézanne which in a marvellous way brings out painterly sensation. Since the self-portrait does not correspond to the anatomical concept of reality, it cannot be called a self-portrait.

The form of the model and the realization are different, leaving only the character, or signs of separate facial features. We see the same divergence, to an ever greater degree, from the point of view of colour.

In the case in point the face is covered with such a colour mass that it could hardly correspond to reality and give the sensation of a body.

'An Attempt to Determine the Relation between Form and Colour in Painting', *Essays on Art*, Vol. 2, edited by Troels Andersen
Trans. by Xenia Glowackacki-Prus and Arnold McMillin, 1968
Originally published 1928–33

## Pablo Picasso (1881–1973), the influential artist of the 20th century

Cézanne was my one and only master! Of course I looked at his paintings... I spent years studying them...Cézanne was like the father of us all.

To Georges Brassaï, 1943
Quoted in Michel Hoog
*Catalogue de l'Exposition Cézanne*
Madrid, 1984

## Pierre Bonnard (1867–1947), French painter and at one time a leading member of the Nabis group

Cézanne, in front of his subject, had a strong idea of what he wanted to do and only took from nature what had a bearing on his idea. It happened that he often remained like a lizard, warming himself in the sun, without even touching a brush. He could wait until things became once more just as they had entered his conception. He was the most powerfully armed painter facing nature, the hardest and the most sincere.

Observations collected by Angèle Lamotte, quoted in *Verve*, 1947

## Max Weber (1881–1961), Russian-born American painter, who was a pioneer in the fields of Fauvism, Cubism and Expressionism

When I saw the first ten pictures by this master, the man who actually, I should say, brought to an end academism, I said to myself as I gazed and looked, after several visits, 'This is the way to paint. This is art *and* nature, reconstructed,' by what I should call today an engineer of the geometry of aesthetics. I came away bewildered. I even changed the use of my brushes. A certain thoughtful hesitance came into my work, and I constantly looked back upon the creative tenacity, this sculpturesque touch of pigment by this great man in finding form, and how he built up his color to construct the form....

Interview 1959
Quoted in John Rewald
*Cézanne and America*, 1989

❛ The master *par excellence* ❜ (Paul Klee). Opposite: *Farmyard at Auvers* (c. 1879).

# 'Truth in painting'

*Cézanne's works are not explained by his life or his artistic influences. Painting gave meaning to this man who doubted himself and worked unceasingly to 'realize' his vision. The French philosopher Maurice Merleau-Ponty retraces the steps of the man who wished to unite art and nature.*

## Cézanne's doubt

He needed a hundred working sessions for a still-life, a hundred and fifty sittings for a portrait. What we call his work was for him only an experiment and an approach to his painting. He wrote in September 1906, aged sixty-seven, one month before his death: 'I am in such a state of mental confusion, in such great agitation that I have feared for my reason for a time... Now I seem to be better and am thinking more precisely about the direction of my studies. Shall I ever arrive at the goal which has been so much sought and so long pursued? I study from nature always and it seems to me that I proceed very slowly.' Painting was his world and his way of life. He worked alone, with no pupils, with no admiration from his family, no encouragement from juries. He even painted the afternoon of his mother's

Landscape of the Midi (c. 1885). 'I must search for the expression of what I feel and organize my feelings into my own personal aesthetic.'

death. In 1870 he painted at l'Estaque while policemen were searching for him as a defaulter [avoiding conscription for the Franco-Prussian War which broke out in the summer].

And yet he got to the point of calling this vocation in question. As he grew old, he wondered whether the innovation of his painting did not come from defective eye-sight, if all his life had not been founded on a chance formation of his body.

## The paradox

His painting is a form of paradox: searching for reality without giving up sensation, without taking any other guide than the immediate impression of nature, without outlining contours, without framing colour in drawing, without composing perspective or the picture. That is what Emile Bernard calls Cézanne's suicide: he aims at reality and forbids himself the means of attaining it. There lies the reason for his difficulties and also for the distortions that are found, especially between 1870 and 1890. Plates or cups placed in profile on a table should be ellipses, but the two apexes of the ellipse grow enlarged and dilated. The work table, in the portrait of Gustave Geffroy [see p. 104b], spreads out in the lower part of the picture against all the laws of perspective.

In abandoning drawing, Cézanne was said to be giving himself up to the chaos of sensations. Now sensations would upset objects and constantly suggest illusions, as they sometimes do – for example the illusion of objects moving when we shake our heads – if judgment did not constantly correct appearances. Cézanne, says Bernard, engulfed 'painting in ignorance and his mind in darkness'.

## To unite art and nature, the senses and the intellect

In his conversations with Emile Bernard, it is obvious that Cézanne is always seeking to escape all the ready-made alternatives being suggested to him – that of the senses or the intellect, of the painter who sees and the painter who thinks, of nature and composition, of primitivism and tradition. 'You have to have a point of view,' he said, but 'by a point of view I mean a logical vision, that's to say nothing absurd.' 'Is it a question of our nature?' asks Bernard. Cézanne replies: 'It is a question of both.'

'Aren't nature and art different?' – 'I would like to unite them. Art is a personal apprehension. I place this apprehension in sensation and I ask the intellect to organize it into a work of art.' But even these formulae make too much room for ordinary ideas of 'sensibility' or 'sensation' and 'intellect'; that is why Cézanne could not convince and why he preferred to paint. Instead of applying dichotomies to his work which belong more to scholastic traditions than to the founders – philosophers or painters – of these traditions, it would be better to be receptive to the real meaning of his painting, which is to call them into question. Cézanne did not believe he had to choose between sensation and thought, as though between chaos and order. He did not wish to separate static things which appear beneath our gaze from their fleeting manner of appearance; he wanted to paint matter in the act of taking on form, order being born through spontaneous organization. He did not make a division between 'the senses' and 'the intellect', but between the spontaneous order of things perceived and the human order of ideas

Mont Sainte-Victoire and Château Noir . Left: a photograph of c. 1935. Right: a painting of 1904–6. 'His pictures give the impression of nature at its source, whereas photographs of the same landscapes suggest the works of man, their convenience, their looming presence.'

and knowledge. We perceive things, we agree about them, they are deep-rooted in us and it is on the basis of this 'nature' that we erect knowledge. It is this primeval world that Cézanne wanted to paint, and that is why his pictures give the impression of nature at its source, whereas photographs of the same landscapes suggest the works of man, their convenience, their looming presence. Cézanne never wished to 'paint like a brute beast', but to put the intellect, ideas, knowledge, perspective and tradition in touch once more with the natural world: to confront, as he said, knowledge 'which issued from it' with nature itself.

Cézanne's experiments in perspective, through their faithfulness to phenomena, laid bare what recent psychology was to define. Our actual experience of perspective, that of our perception, is not geometric or photographic perspective at all: in our perception, nearer objects appear smaller, further-off objects larger than they do in a photograph; just as can be seen in a cinema when a train gets nearer and nearer and grows larger much more

quickly than a real train in the same circumstances....

Cézanne's genius is to arrange the whole picture so that the distortion of perspective ceases to be visible in itself when one looks at it as a whole, and only gives the impression, as in normal vision, of a new order being born, of an object in the act of appearing, in the act of coming together in front of our eyes. In the same way the contour around objects, thought of as a line which surrounds them, does not belong to the visible world but to geometry. If the contour of an apple is marked with a line it is made into a thing, whereas really this contour is the ideal limit to which the sides of the apple escape in depth. If you don't draw any contour, that would mean taking an object's identity away. If you draw one contour only, that would mean sacrificing depth, that is to say the dimension which gives us the thing, not as it were laid out before us, but full of reservations, and like an inexhaustible reality. That is why Cézanne will follow the swelling of an object with modulated colours, and will mark *several* contours with blue lines. The eye, thrown back from one to the other apprehends a contour nascent between them all, just as it does in the perception. There is nothing less arbitrary than those famous distortions which Cézanne was anyway to abandon in his last period from 1890, when he was no longer to fill his canvas with colours and was to give up his constant production of still-lifes.

### 'When the colour achieves richness, the form attains its fullness also'

Drawing ought to grow out of colour, if one wishes the world to be rendered in all its density, for it is a mass without breaks, an organism made of colours, across which the flight of perspective,

contours, straight lines and curving lines settle down like lines of force and the framework of space is formed and vibrates. 'Drawing and colour are not separate at all; in so far as you paint, you draw. The more the colour harmonizes, the more exact the drawing becomes. When the colour achieves richness, the form attains its fullness also.' Cézanne does not seek to *suggest* tactile sensations, which would give form and depth, by colour. In primeval perception, distinctions between touch and sight are unknown. It is the knowledge of the human body which teaches us in the end to distinguish between our senses. The actual experience is not found or made from sense data themselves, but directly presents itself as the centre from which sense data radiate. We *see* the depth, the velvet softness and the hardness of objects. Cézanne even said that the arrangement of colours must carry within it this indivisible whole; otherwise his painting would be an allusion to things and would not render them in their imperious unity, in their presence and in that unsurpassed completeness which is for us all the definition of reality. That is why each brushstroke made had to satisfy infinite conditions, that is why Cézanne used to meditate for perhaps an hour before placing it; it had to 'contain the air, the light, the object, the plan, the character, the drawing, the style', as Emile Bernard said. The expression of that which *exists* is an infinite task.

Maurice Merleau-Ponty
*Sens et non-sens*, 1948

S*elf-portrait* (c. 1880).

# Cézanne's apples

*All his life Cézanne painted apples. Different meanings have been given for their repeated presence in the artist's pictures: as a souvenir of his friendship with Zola, as objects gathered at random from the artist's studio, as a simple motif which allowed the painter to concentrate on technique and form. The art-historian Meyer Schapiro suggests a psychoanalytic interpretation here.*

*Cézanne executed* The Judgment of Paris *from 1883 to 1885: in it an amorous shepherd offers an armful of apples to a young girl. Basing his essay on this painting, doubtless inspired by Cézanne's memories of Latin poetry, Meyer Schapiro associates apples and eroticism in the painter's work.*

## Apples of friendship

Cézanne could more readily respond to this classic pastoral theme, since in his own youth a gift of apples had indeed been a sign of love. In his later years he recalled in conversation that an offering of apples had sealed his great friendship with Zola. At school in Aix Cézanne had shown sympathy for the younger boy who had been ostracized by his fellow-students. Himself impulsive and refractory, Cézanne took a thrashing from the others for defying them and talking to Zola. 'The next day, he brought me a big basket of apples. "Ah! Cézanne's apples," he said with a playful wink, "they go far back...."'

## Apples of love

The central place given to apples in a theme of love invites a question about the emotional ground of his frequent painting of apples. Does not the association here of fruit and nudity permit us to interpret Cézanne's habitual choice of still-life – which means, of course, the apples – as a displaced erotic interest?

One can entertain more readily the idea of links between the painting of apples and sexual fantasy since in Western folklore, poetry, myth, language and religion, the apple has a familiar erotic sense....

Apples are associated – either consciously or unconsciously – with the symbol of love. Above and left (detail): *Still-life with a Plaster Cupid* (c. 1895).

*Fructus* – the word for fruit in Latin – retained from its source the verb *fruor*, the original meaning of satisfaction,

enjoyment, delight. Through its attractive body, beautiful in color, texture and form, by its appeal to all the senses and promise of physical pleasure, the fruit is the natural analogue of ripe human beauty....

## 'I want to conquer Paris with an apple'

In paintings of the apples he was able to express through their more varied colors and groupings a wider range of moods, from the gravely contemplative to the sensual and ecstatic. In this carefully arranged society of perfectly submissive things the painter could project typical relations of human beings as well as qualities of the larger visible world – solitude, contact, accord, conflict, serenity, abundance and luxury – and even states of elation and enjoyment. The habit of working expressively in this way with still-life objects reflects a root attitude that had become fixed at an early point in his career before the apples were a major theme. But from the remark about Paris and the apple we divine the seriousness of Cézanne's special concentration on the fruit that was to serve him as an instrument for the highest achievement. He not only proclaims that his homely rejected self will triumph through a humble object. By connecting his favored theme with the golden apple of myth he gave it a grander sense and alluded also to that dream of sexual fulfilment which Freud and others of his time too readily supposed was a general goal of the artist's sublimating effort.

Meyer Schapiro
'The Apples of Cézanne:
An Essay on the Meaning of Still-life'
1968
Quoted in *Modern Art:
19th and 20th Centuries*, 1978

# The Mont Sainte-Victoire

*Heavy with symbolism, this mountain fascinated Cézanne and the people of Aix. The painter identified with the Mont Sainte-Victoire and appropriated it. It has acquired a new dimension for everyone today: the dimension given by Cézanne.*

### The late Mont Sainte-Victoires

In some of [his last views of the Mont Sainte-Victoire], the canvas is densely coated with overlaid touches of colour through which the forms of the landscape appear barely discernible, a painful reminder of the aged artist's creatives torments – and tenacity. Others – especially in watercolour – possess a delicacy and lyricism which appear infinitely consoling. Employing myriad flame-like strokes of colour Cézanne creates in these a kind of mystic notation – or visual music – to evoke the celestial harmonies of nature. In several oils and watercolours, the artist even inverts the contour of the mountain in a sequence of coloured touches which converge upon the bottom centre of the composition. These afford moving evidence of the indissoluble order which he believed permeated all facets of creation.

One of the last in the *Mont Sainte-Victoire* series.

Most visionary of all, however, are those late views of the mountain floating weightlesly over the plain, like some spiritual intercessor between man and the divine. In certain of these the hues of the land are discharged into the sky, with Cézanne wringing from them all earthly impurity and permitting them simply to ascend, ecstatic affirmations of both human aspiration and universal harmony. Works such as these communicate a mystical belief in the transcendent beauty of creation which justifies Rilke's assertion that Cézanne set himself before a landscape 'drawing religion from it'.

Richard Verdi<br>
Cézanne, 1992

## Seeing the mountain as it is

The Mont Sainte-Victoire is not the highest point of Provence but, they say, the most precipitous. It does not consist of a single summit but is a long chain whose crest follows an almost straight line at a constant height of about a thousand metres. It does not look like an abrupt peak except when seen from below in the Aix basin, which is about half a day's walk to the west: what appears from there to be the real summit is only the beginning of the crest that extends another half day's walk to the east.

This chain which rises in a gentle slope to the north, and falls away almost vertically from the plateau to the south, is a powerful calcareous fold whose ridge is the upper longtitudinal axis. Seen from the west, these three points take on a dramatic appearance, for they represent in many ways a cross-section of the whole massif and of its various folds, to such an extent that anyone who knew nothing about this mountain would be able to guess its origin, even without

wanting to, and would see there something exceptional....

What is so astonishing and so strange about the Mont Sainte-Victoire is especially the brightness and dolomitic glare of the limestone, 'a rock of the highest quality' as a brochure for mountaineers said. There is no road. The whole mountain and even the very gentle north slope are devoid of any road suitable for motor vehicles and any inhabited house (though there is still an abandoned 17th-century priory on the crest). The steep flank is only accessible to mountaineers; but all the other sides can be climbed without difficulty and one can continue for a long way still on the crest. Even from the nearest village it is a whole day's undertaking.

That July day when I was going eastwards along the Paul Cézanne road, I had barely left Aix when I began to toy with the idea of giving travel advice to a crowd of unknown people (and yet I was only one of many who had followed this route from the beginning of the century). It had long been a game to see the mountain as it really was. Perhaps this cherished motif of a painter had already become something of an idée fixe. It was only on the day when the idea with which I was toying suddenly took over my imagination that all at once the resolution was made (accompanied at once by a feeling of pleasure): yes, I was going to see the Mont Sainte-Victoire close to! And thus it was that I set out, not so much on the track of the exact features that Cézanne had seen, for I knew, after all, that most of them had been altered subsequently, but rather I followed my feelings: it was the mountain that was drawing me as nothing else in my life had drawn me.

Peter Handke<br>
Die Lehre der Sainte-Victoire, 1980

# FURTHER READING

## Standard catalogues of Cézanne's work

Chappuis, Adrien, *The Drawings of Paul Cézanne: A Catalogue Raisonné*, 2 vols., 1973

Cherpin, Jean, *L'Oeuvre gravé de Cézanne*, 1972

Orienti, Sandra, *The Complete Paintings of Cézanne*, 1985

Rewald, John, *Paul Cézanne: The Watercolours*, 1983

Venturi, Lionello, *Cézanne, son art, son oeuvre*, 2 vols., 1936

## Primary sources

Denvir, Bernard (ed.), *The Impressionists at First Hand*, 1987

Doran P.-M., *Conversations avec Cézanne,* 1978

*Joachim Gasquet's Cézanne: A Memoir with Conversations*, trans. Christopher Pemberton, 1991 (original 1921)

Kendall, Richard (ed.), *Cézanne by Himself: Drawings, Paintings, Writings*, 1988

Larguier, Léo, *Le Dimanche avec Paul Cézanne: souvenirs*, 1925

Rewald, John (ed.), *Paul Cézanne Letters* (4th ed.), trans. Marguerite Kay, 1976

Rilke, Rainer Maria, *Letters on Cézanne*, ed. Clara Rilke and trans. Joel Agee, 1985

Rivière, Georges, *Le Maître Paul Cezanne*, 1923

—, *Cézanne, le peintre solitaire*, 1933

Vollard, Ambroise, *Cézanne*, 1984 (original 1914)

Wechsler, Judith, *Cézanne in Perspective*, 1975

## Principal general studies

Barnes, Albert C. and Violette de Mazia, *The Art of Cézanne*, 1939

Bullen, J. B. (ed.), *Post-Impressionists in England: The Critical Reception*, 1988

Dorival, Bernard, *Cézanne*, 1948

Dunlop, Ian, *The Complete Paintings of Cézanne*, 1985

Hoog, Michel, *L'Univers de Cézanne*, 1971

Kendall, Richard, *Cézanne* in *The History and Techniques of the Great Masters*, 1989

—, *Cézanne by Himself: Drawings, Paintings, Writings*, 1988

Mack, Gerstle, *Cézanne*, 1989

Rewald, John, *Cézanne: A Biography*, 1986

Schapiro, Meyer, *Paul Cézanne*, 1988

—, *Modern Art: 19th and 20th Centuries*, 1978

Schiff, Richard, *Cézanne and the End of Impressionism: A Study of the Theory, Technique and Critical Evaluation of Modern Art*, 1984

Venturi, Lionello, *Cézanne*, 1978

Verdi, Richard, *Cézanne*, 1992

—, *Cézanne and Poussin: The Classical Vision of Landscape*, 1990

## Monographs and specialized studies

Anderson, W., *Cézanne's Portrait Drawings*, 1970

Arrouye, Jean, *La Provence de Cézanne*, 1982

Badt, Kurt, *The Art of Cézanne*, 1985

Barskaya, Anna, *Paul Cézanne: Paintings from the Museums of the Soviet Union*, 1983

Berthold, Gertrude, *Cézanne und die alten Meister*, 1958

Brion-Guerry, Liliane, *Cézanne et l'expression de l'espace*, 1966

Fry, Roger, *Cézanne: A Study of his Development*, 1989 (original 1927)

Geffroy, Gustave, *Claude Monet, sa vie, son oeuvre*, 1924

Lewis, Mary Tompkins, *Cézanne's Early Imagery*, 1989

Loran, Erle, *Cézanne's Composition*, 1943

Malevich, Kazimir, *Essays on Art*, trans. Xenia Glowackacki-Prus and Arnold McMillin, 1968 (original 1928–33)

McLeave, Hugh, *A Man and his Mountain: The Life of Cézanne*, 1977

Niess, Robert Judson, *Zola, Cézanne, and Manet: A Study of 'L'Oeuvre'*, 1968

Novotny, Fritz, *Cézanne und das Ende der wissenschaftlichen Perspektive*, 1938

Rewald, John, *Cézanne and America: Dealers, Collectors, Artists and Critics 1891–1921*, 1989

—, *Cézanne, The Steins and Their Circle*, 1986

—, *Paul Cézanne: The Watercolours*, 1983

Zola, Emile, *The Masterpiece*, trans. Thomas Walton, 1950

## Exhibition catalogues

*Cézanne*, Edinburgh and London, The Tate Gallery, 1954

*Cézanne dans les musées nationaux*, Orangerie des Tuileries, Paris, 1974

Gowing, Sir Lawrence, *Cézanne: The Early Years 1859–1872*, Royal Academy of Arts, London, 1988

Krumrine, Mary Louise, *Paul Cézanne: The Bathers*, Kunstmuseum, Basle, 1989 (English edition 1990)

*Paul Cézanne*, Museo Español de Arte Contemporaneo, Madrid, 1984

Rishel, Joseph J., *Cézanne in Philadelphia Collections*, Philadelphia Museum of Art, 1983

Rubin, William (ed.), *Cézanne: The Late Work*, The Museum of Modern Art, New York 1977; Museum of Fine Arts, Houston; Galeries Nationales du Grand Palais, Paris

Sterling, Charles, *Cézanne*, Musée de l'Orangerie, Paris, 1936

# LIST OF ILLUSTRATIONS

*All works are by Paul Cézanne unless stated otherwise.*

The following abbreviations have been used:
*a* above, *b* below, *c* centre, *l* left, *r* right.

## COVER

**Front** *Self-portrait* (detail). c. 1875. Oil on canvas, 64 x 53 cm. Musée d'Orsay, Paris
**Spine** *Fruit, Napkin and Milk-can* (detail). 1879–82. Oil on canvas, 60 x 73 cm. Walter-Guillaume Collection. Musée de l'Orangerie, Paris
**Back** *Mont Sainte-Victoire, Seen from Bibémus Quarry*. c. 1897. Oil on canvas, 65 x 81 cm. Baltimore Museum of Art

## OPENING

**1** *The Red Rock*. c. 1900. Oil on canvas, 91 x 66 cm. Musée de l'Orangerie, Paris
**2–9** Details of *The Red Rock*. Photographs by Pierre Pitrou

## CHAPTER 1

**11** *Apples and Biscuits* (detail). 1879–82. Oil on canvas, 46 x 55 cm. Walter-Guillaume Collection. Musée de l'Orangerie, Paris
**12** *Self-portrait*. 1861–2. Oil on canvas, 44 x 37 cm. Private collection
**13** Paul Cézanne c. 1861. Photograph
**14l** *Portrait of Marie Cézanne*. c. 1866. Oil on canvas, 53.5 x 37 cm. The Saint Louis Art Museum
**14r** *Uncle Dominique* or *The Man in the Cotton Bonnet*. 1866. Oil on canvas, 79.7 x 64.1 cm. The Metropolitan Museum of Art, New York
**15l** A postcard of Aix-en-Provence dating from the beginning of the 20th century
**15r** Collège Bourbon, Aix-en-Provence
**16a** *Study of Nudes Diving*. c. 1863–6. Drawing. Mr and Mrs Harrison Collection, Los Angeles County Museum of Art, Los Angeles
**16b** *Femme piquant une tête dans l'eau*. c. 1867–70. Pencil, watercolour and gouache on paper 12.7 x 12.1 cm. National Museum of Wales, Cardiff
**17a** Louis-Auguste Cézanne. c. 1880. Photograph
**17b** Joseph Gibert. Photograph
**18** Salon of the Jas de Bouffan. c. 1900. Photograph
**19l** *Autumn*. 1860–2. Oil on canvas, 314 x 109 cm. Musée du Petit Palais, Paris
**19r** *Spring*. 1860–2. Oil on canvas, 314 x 109 cm. Musée du Petit Palais, Paris
**20** Drawing in a letter to Zola of 17 January 1859
**21a** Emile Zola aged thirty years old. Photograph

**21c** *Portrait of Delacroix*. 1864–6. Black pencil, 14 x 13 cm. Musée Calvet, Avignon
**21b** Letter from Cézanne to Zola. Private collection
**22a** *Head of an Old Man*. 1865–8. Oil on canvas, 51 x 48 cm. Musée d'Orsay, Paris
**22bl** *Medea and her Children*, after Delacroix. 1879–82. Oil on canvas. Kunsthaus, Zurich
**22br** *The Painter*. c. 1868–71. Pencil, 17 x 10 cm. Kunstmuseum, Basle
**23** *Portrait of Antony Valabrègue*. c. 1869. Oil on canvas, 60 x 50 cm. The J. Paul Getty Museum, Malibu, California
**24l** Manet. *Le Déjeuner sur l'Herbe*. 1863. Oil on canvas, 208 x 264 cm. Musée d'Orsay, Paris
**24r** The Salon des Refusés. Comic drawing in *Le Charivari*, 20 May 1863
**25** *The Murder*. c. 1867–8. Oil on canvas, 64 x 81 cm. The National Museums and Galleries on Merseyside, Walker Art Gallery, Liverpool
**26–7** *Paul Alexis Reading to Zola*. 1869–70. Oil on canvas, 131 x 161 cm. Art Museum, Sao Paulo, Brazil
**27br** Edouard Manet. *Portrait of Emile Zola*. 1868. Oil on canvas, 146 x 114 cm. Musée d'Orsay, Paris
**28** and **28–9a** and **28–9b** (details) *Portrait of Louis-Auguste Cézanne, the Artist's Father, Reading l'Evénement*. 1866. Oil on canvas, 200 x 120 cm. Collection of Mr and Mrs Paul Mellon, National Gallery of Art, Washington, D.C.
**28–9a** *Still-life with Sugar Bowl, Pears and Blue Cup*. 1863–5. Oil on canvas, 30 x 41 cm. Musée Granet, Aix-en-Provence
**30** *Portrait of Achille Emperaire*. c. 1868–70. Charcoal and lead pencil, 49 x 31 cm. Musée du Louvre, Département des Arts Graphiques, Paris
**31** *Portrait of Achille Emperaire*. 1866–70. Oil on canvas, 200 x 122 cm. Musée d'Orsay, Paris
**32l** *Christ in Limbo*. c. 1867. Oil on canvas, 165 x 124 cm. Private collection
**32r** *Mary Magdalene* or *Sorrow*. c. 1867. Oil on canvas, 165 x 124 cm. Musée d'Orsay, Paris
**33al** *Marion and Valabrègue Setting out to Paint from Nature*. 1866. Oil on canvas, 39 x 31 cm. Private collection
**33ar** Fortuné Marion. c. 1866. Photograph
**33b** *Landscape at Aix*. 1865–7. Oil on canvas, 28 x 35 cm. Pierre Lévy Collection, Musée de Troyes
**34** *The Orgy* or *The Feast*. c. 1870. Oil on canvas, 130 x 81 cm. Private collection
**35** *The Abduction* or *The Rape*. 1867. Oil on canvas, 90 x 117 cm. The Provost and Fellows of King's College, Cambridge
**36** *Still-life with Skull and Candlestick*. 1865–7. Oil on canvas, 47.5 x 62.5 cm. Private collection, Zurich

## CHAPTER 2

## CHAPTER 3

CHAPTER 4

## DOCUMENTS

# INDEX

# TEXT CREDITS

Grateful acknowledgment is made for use of material from the following works: (pp. 35, 140) John Rewald, *Cézanne: A Biography*, copyright © 1986 Harry N. Abrams, B. V., The Netherlands; reprinted by permission of Harry N. Abrams, Inc., New York. (pp. 136–7) *Cézanne by Himself*, edited by Richard Kendall, 1988; reprinted by permission of Little, Brown and Company (UK) Ltd, London. (pp. 109, 119) John Rewald, *Cézanne: The Late Work*, edited by William Rubin, The Museum of Modern Art, New York, 1977, copyright © 1977 by The Museum of Modern Art, New York, painting entries in catalog copyright © 1977 by John Rewald, watercolor entries copyright © 1977 by Adrien Chappuis and John Rewald; reprinted by permission of The Museum of Modern Art and John Rewald. (p. 158) Kazimir Malevich, 'An Attempt to Determine the Relation between Form and Colour in Painting', *Essays on Art*, Vol. 2, edited by Troels Andersen, trans. by Xenia Glowackacki-Prus and Arnold McMillin, 1968, copyright © 1968 Borgens Forlag A/S; reprinted by permission of Borgens Forlag A/S, Valby, Denmark. (pp. 164–5) Meyer Schapiro, 'The Apples of Cézanne: An Essay on the Meaning of Still-life', *Modern Art: 19th and 20th Centuries*, Chatto and Windus Ltd, London, 1978, copyright © Meyer Schapiro 1968; reprinted by permission of Chatto and Windus Ltd, London, the Estate of Meyer Schapiro and George Braziller, Inc., New York; (p. 121) Meyer Schapiro, *Cézanne*, 1988, reprinted by permission of Harry N. Abrams, Incorporated, New York.

# PHOTO CREDITS

Agraci, Paris 97a. Albright-Knox Art Gallery, Buffalo 51–2b. All rights reserved 33al, 36–7, 101a, 101b, 130, 162l. Artephot 149. Artephot/Babey 36, 122bl, 122br. Artephot/Bridgeman Art Library 34, 45l, 84–5, 90br, 91b, 94, 98a, 98c, 98b, 111al, 120–1. Artephot/Cercle d'Art 86a. Artephot/Faillet 22bl, 97b. Artephot/Held 41, 60, 90bc, 91b, 105, 106, 125al, 125b. Artephot/Hinz Colorphoto 90a. Artephot/J. Martin 46–7a. Artephot/Nimatallah 65a, 86b, 136–7. Artephot/Trela 21b, 45r, 141. Art Institute of Chicago 52b, 111ar, 163. Baltimore Museum of Art back cover. Barnes Foundation, Merion, Pennsylvania 99a, 117a. Bibliothèque Nationale, Paris 18, 24r, 46–7b, 131, 135, 159. Bridgestone Museum of Art, Tokyo 162r. Brouchian F., Aix-en-Provence 50a. Bulloz, Paris 19l, 19r, 150. Colombus Museum of Art, Ohio 50b. Courtauld Institute Galleries, London 100a, 164, 165. Dagli Orti, Paris 26–7. Edimédia, Paris 56, 68–9, 89ar, 102–3. The Fitzwilliam Museum, Cambridge 67. Fogg Art Museum, Cambridge, Mass. 42, 43. Galerie Bernheim Jeune, Paris 129. Galerie Louise Leiris, Paris 155. Galerie Schmidt, Paris 160. Giraudon, Paris 90bl, 91ca, 145. Harlingue-Viollet, Paris 21a. The Harvard University Art Museums, Cambridge, Mass. 74–5, 77a. Heald David 46l. Henry Ely, Aix-en-Provence 87, 96–7. Josse, Paris 79. Kunstmuseum, Basle 55, 60–1, 76–7, 77, 78–9, 89cr, 92b, 117b. Lauros/Giraudon 104a, 118–9, 124, 138. Memorial Art Gallery, Rochester, New York 55b. The Metropolitan Museum of Art, New York 14r, 88, 99b. Musée Calvet, Avignon 21c. Museum Boymans van Beuningen, Rotterdam 44c, 65b. Museum of Art, Philadelphia 66r. The Museum of Fine Arts, Boston, Mass. 40bl, 128. The Museum of Modern Art, New York 108–9, 111b. National Gallery of Art, Washington, D. C. 122a. The National Museums and Galleries on Merseyside, Walker Art Gallery, Liverpool 25. Nationalmuseum, Stockholm, 103. The National Museum of Wales, Cardiff 16b. The J. Paul Getty Museum, Malibu, California 23. Philadelphia Museum of Art 125c. Réunion des Musées Nationaux, Paris front cover, l, 2–9, 11, 12, 22a, 24l, 27br, 29, 30, 31, 32r, 33ar, 44l, 45c, 48, 49a, 49bl, 49br, 52–3a, 53b, 57, 58–9, 61c, 61r, 62, 63, 64, 66l, 70, 71, 72–3, 80–1, 82, 83, 89, 89b, 92a, 93, 95, 98, 100b, 102l, 102r, 104b, 110, 139, 146, 151, 157, 158, 166. The Saint Louis Art Museum, Saint Louis 14l. Scala, Florence 38, 39, 112–3, 114–5, 126–7. Sipa Icono 106–7. Sirot-Angel, Paris 78, 116, 133, 135, 150. Terlay B., Aix-en-Provence 15, 20, 144. Thyssen-Bornemisza Collection, Lugano 123.

Michel Hoog
is the Chief Curator at the Musée de l'Orangerie, Paris.
He has organized several exhibitions, amongst them
*Robert Delaunay* (Musée de l'Orangerie in Paris, 1976);
*Realism and Poetry in Russian Painting of the 19th Century*
(Grand Palais in Paris,
National Gallery of Canada at Ottawa,
Californian Palace of the Legion of Honor at San Francisco,
1982–3);
*Le Douanier Rousseau* (Grand Palais in Paris,
Museum of Modern Art in New York, 1984).
His publications include: *Peinture Moderne* (1969);
*Robert Delaunay* (1976);
*Claude Monet, Les Nymphéas* (1984),
which received the Bernier Prize from the Institute;
*Gauguin, Life and Work*, 1987.
Most of these books have
been translated into several languages.
Michel Hoog has been professor at
the Ecole du Louvre since 1971.

© Gallimard/Réunion des musées nationaux 1989

English translation © Thames and Hudson Ltd, London,
and Harry N. Abrams, Inc., New York, 1994

Reprinted 1999

Translated by Rosemary Stonehewer

British Library Cataloguing-in-Publication Data

A catalogue record for this book is available from
the British Library

ISBN 0–500–30037–2

Printed and bound in Italy
by Editoriale Libraria, Trieste